THE CONTRADICTORY ALLIANCE:

STATE-LABOR RELATIONS AND
REGIME CHANGE IN MEXICO

RESEARCH SERIES / NUMBER 83

THE CONTRADICTORY ALLIANCE:

STATE-LABOR RELATIONS AND
REGIME CHANGE IN MEXICO

Ruth Berins Collier

UNIVERSITY OF CALIFORNIA AT BERKELEY

Chapters 1 and 2 contain material published in Ruth Berins Collier and David Collier, *Shaping the Political Arena: Critical Junctures, the Labor Movement, and Regime Dynamics in Latin America* (Princeton: Princeton University Press, 1991). They are used by permission of the publisher.

Cover photo by Greg Smith.

Library of Congress Cataloging-in-Publication Data

Collier, Ruth Berins.
    The contradictory alliance : state-labor relations and regime change in Mexico / Ruth Berins Collier.
        p. cm. — (Research series ; no. 83)
    Includes bibliographical references and index.
    ISBN 0-87725-183-5 (paper) : $14.50 (est.)
    1. Mexico—Politics and government—20th century. 2. Mexico—Politics and government—1970–1988. 3. Labor movement—Mexico—History—20th century. I. Title. II. Series: Research series (University of California, Berkeley. International and Area Studies) ; no. 83.
JL1281.C65 1992
322'.2'0972—dc20   91-46976
                                                         CIP

To the memory of my father, Maurice H. Berins,
for his integrity, humanity, and love

CONTENTS

ACKNOWLEDGMENTS

I would like to acknowledge the assistance of the many people who have contributed to the preparation of this study. I owe very special gratitude to two colleagues who have offered support over many years and in many ways: Carl Rosberg, former director of the Institute of International Studies, and Alex Saragoza, chair of the Center for Latin American Studies, both at the University of California at Berkeley, have been as generous in the time and energy expended on my behalf as in the personal encouragement they have given me. In addition, I would like to acknowledge the financial support of both the Institute of International Studies and the Center for Latin American Studies, which sponsored this study.

In thinking about the current changes in Mexico, I have benefited from the friendship and ongoing conversations with Esthela Gutiérrez Garza and Jorge Castañeda. I also want to acknowledge friends and colleagues who share my enthusiasm for the study of Mexican politics and who have taken the time to give me comments on the manuscript: John Bailey, Roderic Camp, David Collier, Maria Lorena Cook, Michael Foley, Raul Hinojosa, and Robert Kaufman. Yemile Mizrahi and Juan Molinar Horcasitas generously shared data and information with me.

Bojana Ristich achieved the impossible: with consummate skill, equanimity, and flexibility, she made the process of copy-editing and publication a pleasant one. Sara Schatz and Pierre Ostiguy were valuable and energetic research assistants. With forbearance and perception, Peter Houtzager ably prepared the index. Jill Roberts also provided energetic and skillful assistance, and Sue and Greer Allen were, as ever, warmly generous with design advice, as was Christine Taylor.

With the permission of Princeton University Press, Chapters 1 and 2 contain materials that were published in *Shaping the Political Arena: Critical Junctures, the Labor Movement, and Regime Dynamics in Latin America*. Readers are referred there for a more detailed discussion of the critical juncture framework, the early period of Mexican politics, and a comparative analysis of pre-1982 Mexican politics in relation to other Latin American countries.

I owe special thanks to my family, David, Jennifer, and Stephen. In addition to the usual kinds of support, understanding, and love for which families are commonly acknowledged, their resilience and good humor made it possible for me to see this manuscript through the final editing stages in the months following the devastation of the Oakland fire.

R. B. C.

Berkeley, California
March 1992

Chapter I

INTRODUCTION

In the second half of the 1980s, movements for democratization swept through the world. In Latin America, military rule was replaced by civilian regimes. The trend started in Peru in 1980 and went on to include Argentina, Brazil, Uruguay, even Paraguay, and finally, by the end of the decade, Chile. Elsewhere, in the Philippines and Korea, dictators were either overthrown or forced to initiate a political transformation or opening. In yet other regions, countries characterized by one-party rule began similar processes of transformation and opening, with very different degrees of pressure from popular opposition movements. These ranged from Communist one-party regimes of the Soviet Union and Eastern Europe to anti-Communist regimes like Taiwan. The explanation for the era of global political opening is complex, and its links to international economic change will have to await careful comparative analysis. Here I would like to explore the source and significance of current changes in Mexico.

The question of democratization was posed most dramatically in the one-party regime of Mexico in 1988. In elections that July, the ruling Partido Revolucionario Institucional (PRI), according to many analyses, either lost the presidency to the new Frente Democrático Nacional (FDN) or at most managed a small plurality. Even official electoral returns, clearly marked by fraud but corresponding closely to pre-election opinion polls, claimed only the barest majority for the ruling party, which in the decades since its founding had never failed to win an election by overwhelming margins.

Unlike most countries of Latin America, whose twentieth-century history was punctuated by military coups and characterized by unstable political structures, post-revolutionary Mexico, at least until the 1980s, had a stable one-party hegemonic regime. While many observers have emphasized the impressive cooptive capacity and flexibility of the Mexican regime, enabling it to defeat whatever

1

opposition arose, others have been proclaiming its demise since at least the 1970s. Following the 1988 elections, most voices—including those skeptical of previous projections of fundamental change—were added to the funereal chorus, so momentous did those events seem. Yet as the post-election euphoria receded, the nature of the change remained difficult to determine.

What kind of watershed is this current period in Mexico? Any interpretation must be seen against the larger backdrop of Mexican twentieth-century history. That history is one not only of stability and continuity since the 1910–17 revolution, as is widely stated, but also of stability with change—both with institutional flexibility and adaptability and even with moments of dramatic change and challenges to the contours of the system. It is this combination of change and continuity, or even change qua continuity, which has made the Mexican picture so puzzling.

This study provides a framework for interpreting the post-revolutionary evolution of the Mexican political system. Specifically, I look at Mexico within what may be called a critical juncture perspective (Collier and Collier 1991). The Mexican regime is commonly seen as having its origins in the years of post-revolutionary consolidation, roughly from the Constitution of 1917 to the populist reforms of Lázaro Cárdenas between 1934 and 1940. This critical juncture of political reorientation will be examined, and the one-party hegemonic regime that is its legacy will provide a baseline against which change and the possibility of a new critical juncture in the 1980s can be assessed.

The critical juncture framework presents a model of discontinuous or punctuated political change and emphasizes the importance of historical watersheds, or what might loosely be called "founding moments," when new political structures and institutions are established. Often such political reorientation occurs in response to socioeconomic change, which ultimately produces basic political changes in class and sectoral alliances. These, in turn, come to be reflected in changes in the party system and the nature of the political regime. The resulting new political institutions and arrangements are seen as having their own dynamics, which influence much of the subsequent pattern of political change. Thus, although socioeconomic change may be a cause of the political reorientation, between these junctures the political sphere may be characterized by substantial autonomy, due to both the impact of a political logic or dynamic that self-propels political arrangements or defines the parameters of their evolution, and institutional rigidities, sunk costs, and vested interests that act to perpetuate existing structures and resist fundamental change. Nevertheless, with its emphasis on periods of political founding and change, the critical juncture model highlights the possibility that eventually further socioeconomic change will create new pressures on the political regime as key groups or social sectors perceive it to be inconsistent with their evolving goals and interests. The model is thus useful for examining not only political change and continuity, but also the political impact of socioeconomic change and a more autonomous political logic.

In this framework, Latin American political regimes by mid-twentieth century can be understood as an outcome of the way these countries met a set of earlier political challenges posed by fundamental socioeconomic changes that took place in the course of modernization and industrialization in the late nineteenth and early twentieth centuries. At the most general level, these changes consisted of economic expansion and the rise of new social classes. More specifically, the growth of new urban commercial and industrial activities, at first partly a spinoff of the export boom in primary products, gave rise to two new social categories: a working class and a more heterogeneous set of groups commonly referred to as the "middle sectors."* These socioeconomic changes produced new issues and political cleavages.

One line of cleavage was between the traditional oligarchy, who controlled the laissez-faire state, and the new middle sectors, who wanted not only to wrest control of the state, but also to transform it into a more activist state that would play a more interventionist role in social and economic matters. Another line of cleavage was between employers and workers in the commercial and industrial sectors. This conflict put on the political agenda demands for the establishment of an institutionalized mechanism for the resolution of capital-labor disputes which involved the legalization of an organized labor movement and a labor law that defined the terms and conditions of an industrial relations system. Once middle-sector

*The "middle sectors" refers to members of a broad range of urban modern sector occupational groups whose "position" is between the working class and the traditional oligarchy.

representatives took control of the state from the traditional oligarchy, a major issue was the incorporation of the working class into
the political system. Throughout Latin America this incorporation
project constituted a critical juncture that produced a legacy of class
alliances, political coalitions, party configurations, and regime characteristics (see Figure 1).*

In Mexico, the incorporation project, a type that may be labeled
radical populism, included the peasantry as well as the labor movement. Based on the mobilization of popular support, it was characterized by the formation of a multiclass governing coalition that
included labor, and its outcome was the one-party dominant, integrative, hegemonic regime based on popular-sector support. Formal
linkages between labor organizations and the governing party institutionalized the working-class constituency of the party and the
state-labor alliance that underlay the legitimacy of the regime.

Many different perspectives may of course be employed to
analyze the current period of Mexican politics. This critical juncture
framework seems particularly appropriate in part because it focuses
on potential political discontinuities. In addition, it highlights many
significant issues of particular relevance to the present: the political
impact of socioeconomic change, the centrality of labor in political
coalitions and regime dynamics, and the issue of the continuity of
or change in the legacy of the critical juncture. In the 1980s and 1990s,
as in the earlier period, Mexico has been feeling the impact of major
socioeconomic change, the coalitional position of labor has again
become central, and the issue of the continuity or change in the
regime that was the legacy of the earlier critical juncture has become
relevant not only for analysts, but also for both government and
opposition in Mexican politics. In short, the question of a new critical
juncture and another fundamental reorientation of Mexican politics
has arisen, and this perspective provides not only a framework, but
also a baseline for analysis.

If the earlier critical juncture was associated with economic
growth in the early stages of national industrialization, the current
period is associated with a process of economic reorientation in the
later stages of industrialization involving the internationalization of
production. The reorganization of production on a global scale, the

*This argument has been extensively elaborated on the basis of a comparative
analysis of eight Latin American countries in Collier and Collier (1991).

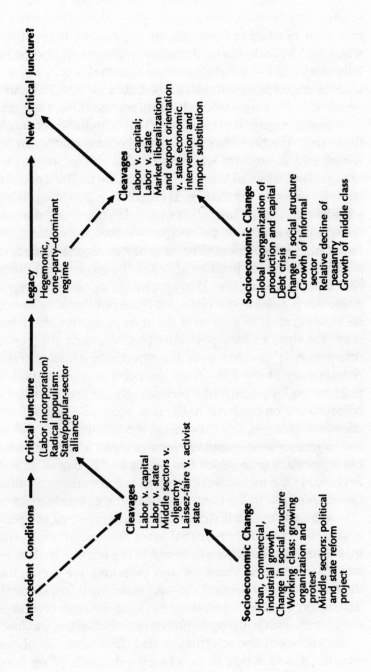

Figure 1

CRITICAL JUNCTURE FRAMEWORK

Antecedent Conditions → Critical Juncture → Legacy → New Critical Juncture?

Cleavages
Labor v. capital
Labor v. state
Middle sectors v. oligarchy
Laissez-faire v. activist state

Critical Juncture
(Labor incorporation)
Radical populism:
State/popular-sector alliance

Legacy
Hegemonic, one-party–dominant regime

Cleavages
Labor v. capital;
Labor v. state
Market liberalization and export orientation v. state economic intervention and import substitution

Socioeconomic Change
Urban, commercial, industrial growth
Change in social structure
Working class: growing organization and protest
Middle sectors: political and state reform project

Socioeconomic Change
Global reorganization of production and capital
Debt crisis
Change in social structure
Growth of informal sector
Relative decline of peasantry
Growth of middle class

logic of both international competitiveness and international integration, and the harsh constraints of the debt crisis have combined to
fundamentally reorient economies throughout the world. The question, then, is whether these economic changes will constitute a major
watershed in which Latin American politics will also be fundamentally reoriented—i.e., whether these economic changes are consistent
with or contradictory to established alliance patterns and the party
systems and regimes which institutionalize these alliances.

In this regard, it is interesting that with these economic changes
the "labor question" has once again become central. In Mexico the
earlier critical juncture was associated with the political integration
of organized labor; in the current period the political position of labor
is under pressure for change. The earlier critical juncture established
a broad political coalition that included organized labor, institutionalized that coalition in the one-party dominant system, and laid the
foundation for an integrative, hegemonic regime. The regime resulting from the earlier juncture afforded the government many political
resources, including even the capacity to pursue the unpopular liberal
economic policies of the 1980s. Yet these policies have been detrimental to labor, reversing much of the state protection that labor enjoyed
from the time of incorporation. To this extent the new economic
orientation is at odds with the governing alliance and the labor
constituency of the PRI—from the point of view of both labor and
political leaders, who find it increasingly difficult to maintain a labor
constituency on the basis of the new economic policies. The current
economic changes, therefore, seem inconsistent with the older political outcomes or accommodations—indeed with a salient feature of
the Mexican regime which has been a key source of its stability and
hegemony: the inclusion of labor in the governing coalition and its
central position in the constituency of the governing party.

Whereas the earlier critical juncture involved the political integration of a national organized labor movement, the current period
may lead to its "denationalization," in the sense of both its integration
into a larger world economy and pressures for decoupling it from
the national governing alliance and reducing it to a sectoral or plant-
level actor. Thus, as noted, labor has again become pivotal: it presents
state actors with both opportunities and challenges, and labor, in turn,
is torn between the advantages and disadvantages of cooperating
with the state. Political leaders face the dilemma of, on the one hand,

continuing to rely on the unusual governmental capacity that has derived from labor support—even to pursue in the short-run policies that are unfavorable to labor—or, on the other, pursuing such policies in a longer-run economic restructuring that may cause the forfeiting of labor support. At the same time, labor faces its traditional dilemma of trying to protect its interests from either inside the governing coalition or from overt opposition. These alternatives are at the core of the current political dynamic in Mexico.

In order to provide a base from which to assess the current political changes, it is necessary to understand the origins and characteristics of the regime that was in place prior to the 1980s. Against this backdrop, we can then raise the question of the extent to which the events surrounding 1988 represent a decisive break with earlier patterns—i.e., whether the current changes represent a limited political adjustment or a more fundamental political reorientation, a new critical juncture which is bringing about a new set of alliances—particularly with respect to organized labor—and a new type of regime.

In this analysis we shall first review the initial incorporation of labor in Mexico as the critical juncture in which, following the 1910–17 revolution, the oligarchic state was replaced by a new activist state and a new period of mass politics was inaugurated. A "revolutionary coalition" of organized labor, as well as an organized peasantry, was institutionalized in an inclusionary party regime. We shall describe the evolving strategy of political leaders in forging and maintaining the coalition with labor in order to consolidate power and establish a legitimate political order, along with the evolution of that coalition from radical populism to one with a more subordinate position for labor.

Against this background, we shall next focus on politics in the decade following the 1982 debt crisis to explore the potential impact of the current socioeconomic conjuncture, its coalitional logic, and the challenge to the political structures that have long been in place in Mexican politics. In response to domestic and international economic changes, the government in the 1980s launched economic liberalization policies that created strong pressures on the historic state-labor alliance. In the context of these dilemmas and contradictions, the recent socioeconomic changes have given rise to competing political projects in favor of a more competitive and pluralistic regime—as well as resistance to such changes. PRI reformers, the private sector and opposition groups on the right, and leftist opponents have each put forth political liberalization projects which would sever the long-standing state-labor alliance. That different groups see political liberalization as a means of either furthering or opposing economic liberalization emphasizes some of the ambiguities of this political change. Accordingly, many of these groups are also ambivalent about it, responding to contingencies as they arise.

We shall thus consider the changes that occurred in the 1980s in terms of the contradictory pressures for sustaining or disarticulating the coalition with labor—that is, for continuing the legacy of the earlier critical juncture or restructuring politics in Mexico.

Chapter 2

THE CRITICAL JUNCTURE:
FOUNDING THE MEXICAN REGIME

THE MEXICAN INCORPORATION PERIOD IN
COMPARATIVE PERSPECTIVE

Between the 1940s and the 1980s, Mexico had a hegemonic, semi-competitive civilian regime whose stability was unusual in comparison with the experience of most other countries in Latin America. As noted, the origins of this regime may be found in the period of post-revolutionary consolidation from the 1917 Constitution through the Cárdenas presidency from 1934 to 1940. This interval corresponded to a critical juncture that was pivotal in regime evolution throughout Latin America: the initial incorporation of organized labor as a legitimate social actor. In Mexico, the incorporation extended to the peasantry as well in the context of rural mobilization during the Mexican Revolution.

Throughout Latin America, this initial incorporation took place typically in the first decades of the twentieth century in response to the commercial and in some cases also industrial growth that accompanied the boom of primary product exports in the last decades of the nineteenth century. Under the impetus of this growth, two new social sectors were created: a working class in commerce, industry, and sometimes exports (such as mining), and the middle sectors, whose social, economic, and political importance had increased rapidly with the sustained expansion of the export economy and the growth of the urban commercial and manufacturing activities in which they were engaged.

In the context of this socioeconomic change, many pressures arose for a major political reorientation. Some working-class groups espoused a revolutionary project for the transformation of the state. This was not to be successful, though working-class organization and aspirations were a central factor in the political reorientation that did occur. A different political project was undertaken by reformist modernizers more representative of the new middle sectors. A key element of this project, once oligarchic hegemony had been overcome, was the transformation of the state from a laissez-faire state to a more modernizing, interventionist state which would assume new social, welfare, and economic responsibilities.

High on the new agenda was the incorporation of labor as a response to the "social question" posed by new forms of organization of the emerging working class and the protest in which it engaged. Workers demanded higher wages, better working conditions, and the right to strike and bargain collectively. Older patterns of workers' association oriented toward mutual aid societies began to give way to new forms, often inspired by anarcho-syndical and later Communist ideologies. By the first decades of the twentieth century, substantial union movements had appeared in the major Latin American countries, along with dramatic episodes of labor protest and strikes. In the absence of any legal recognition of the right to organize or strike, this new working-class activation and militance was typically met with violent state repression, sometimes involving the deaths of hundreds of workers.

For the state reformers, violent repression was not an appropriate long-term solution. A new mode of state-labor relations was called for in which labor repression would give way to institutionalization and exclusion would give way to incorporation. In conjunction with the new social and welfare responsibilities, the state introduced legislation regulating such things as working conditions, minimum wages, and social security. With the new economic responsibilities, the state began to establish a regularized system of labor relations, assuming a role as mediator of class conflict and arbiter of labor-management disputes. With the legalization of unions and the regulation of a system of collective bargaining and conflict resolution, reformers sought to take the labor question out of the streets and away from the police or army and bring it into the realm of law. To different degrees in the various Latin American countries, these changes were accompanied by the introduction of corporatism as a new structure for the vertical integration of the new economic sectors.*

For the reformist modernizers, the emergence of the working class posed both a challenge and an opportunity. The challenge was to control the working class as a potentially powerful new force in society. The opportunity lay in the possibility of mobilizing workers as an essential base of political support. In the different countries of Latin America, this tension between control and mobilization was resolved differently, and it is this resolution, the particular mix of control and mobilization, that is central in distinguishing types of labor incorporation and the different political coalitions in which labor was involved and hence in producing the different political legacies which can be traced to mid-century and beyond.

In Mexico, this political reorientation grew out of the revolution and civil war of 1910–17. The project that was to emerge out of these upheavals may be labeled radical populism. Arising from the need to consolidate political power after central political authority had broken down and revolutionary generals had set themselves up as local bosses who could raise personal armies, this project was centrally concerned with the mobilization of working-class support. During the course of this project, the working class was mobilized electorally and organized into unions linked to the reformist political movement or party. In addition, in contrast to most other cases in Latin America, this incorporation extended beyond the working class to encompass the peasantry. In this way, a populist alliance was established based on reformist middle sectors, the working class, and the peasantry.

On the one hand, one must understand radical populism as an elite project to establish the political dominance of emerging urban middle sectors. To this end, populism was pursued as part of a political strategy in which the popular sectors were mobilized as a political support base, as a political resource to build a constituency in order to consolidate power. This mobilization did not encourage

---

*Corporatism can be defined as a system of state-union relations characterized by some degree of (1) state structuring of noncompetitive, compulsory interest associations; (2) state subsidy of these groups; and (3) state-imposed constraints on demand-making, leadership, and internal governance (see Collier and Collier 1979).

autonomous mobilization from below, but rather took the form of controlled mobilization from above.

On the other hand, it is important to understand that the very process of support mobilization took on a dynamic of its own. In order to mobilize support successfully, an exchange was necessary in which real concessions were offered for the support sought, for, contrary to many accounts of Latin American populism, the popular sector leaders were not so passive nor so easily duped that they would collaborate without extracting some benefits. The exchange, a fundamental feature of support mobilization, is the source of the political dynamic contained within populism in Mexico and in Latin America more generally. This exchange, while not threatening the basic capitalist orientation of the state and while in fact doing much to coopt the working class (and the peasantry where included), nevertheless involved substantive concessions, the formation of a progressive alliance, and some degree of power-sharing with leaders of the working class. These changes alienated important sectors of society. The result was political polarization as the alienated groups defected from the coalition. Despite efforts of the political elite to maintain the multi-class alliance, it tended to break apart, so that increasingly there was a situation in which a progressive coalition in power was opposed by the dominant economic sectors, which formed a counter-revolutionary or counter-reform alliance.

Genuine populism, then, was not a static or equilibrium condition but contained within it a political dynamic and contradiction that made it most unstable. It must be understood in terms of this contradictory feature: though mobilization was undertaken largely from above, and though in many ways it was a cooptive mechanism, the dynamics of mobilization turned populism in a sufficiently progressive direction to result in political polarization as economically dominant groups went into vehement opposition, a situation that was unsustainable in the context of a capitalist state. This political dynamic of populism, its fundamentally contradictory nature, places in high relief the limits of reform in Latin American capitalist development. It also points to the fundamental political problem of the post-populist period: the resolution of this contradiction—that is, the need to reestablish the support of the dominant economic sectors that were alienated by populism and yet to retain popular support in order to legitimate the regime and establish stable political structures.

The origins of the Mexican one-party hegemonic regime can thus be traced out in two steps: the radical populism of the initial ① *populism* incorporation period and the dynamics that period produced in its ② *dynamics* aftermath. During the incorporation period political leaders in control of the state initiated an alliance with organized labor and an organized peasantry that formed a crucial element in the support base of the state. Though this populist alliance in many ways gave the state a mechanism of control over the popular sectors, it nevertheless stimulated a powerful conservative reaction that became a dominant feature of the aftermath period. During this period of reaction to radical populism, the nature of the alliance was altered and the characteristics of the one-party hegemonic regime took shape. In sum, the politics of incorporation resulted in the establishment of a political alliance between the state and the organized labor movement and the founding of a populist party that embodied that alliance, and the politics of the aftermath further institutionalized that alliance and the dominance of the party, at the same time that it created a large, electoral majority bloc around a centrist policy orientation.*

RADICAL POPULISM IN MEXICO

In Mexico, the collapse of the oligarchic state occurred with the Mexican Revolution of 1910 that overthrew the long-standing dictator Porfirio Díaz and that was renewed in the civil war that raged from the assassination of President Francisco Madero in 1913 until the victory of the Constitutionalist forces in 1916. In the course of the fighting, the Constitutionalists recognized the advantages of mobilizing labor support. In 1914, following the granting of a number of benefits which served to initiate a rapprochement between the

---

*Principal sources used in the analysis in this chapter include the following: Anguiano (1975), Ashby (1967), Brandenburg (1964), Camacho (1976), Carr (1976), Córdova (1972, 1973, 1974, 1976, 1981), Cornelius (1973), Dulles (1961), Fuentes Díaz (1959), Furtak (1974), Garrido (1984), González Casanova (1982), Hamilton (1982), Hernández Chávez (1979), Leal (1976), López Aparicio (1952), Medín (1982), Medina (1978, 1979), J. Meyer et al. (1977), L. Meyer (1978), L. Meyer et al. (1978), Michaels (1966), North and Raby (1977), Rivera Castro (1983), Saragoza (1988).

Constitutionalists and the major labor confederation, a famous pact was struck between the two in which the latter agreed to form six "Red Battalions" of workers to fight for the Constitutionalist cause. In return, the confederation was given (among other things) freedom and support in carrying out union organizing activities throughout the country. The mobilization of the Red Battalions set an important precedent in Mexican politics, and the period of the incorporation of labor which was initiated at the end of the war was centrally concerned with the mobilization of labor support as the new leadership sought to consolidate its power.

Following a first cautious phase from 1917 to 1920, the Mexican incorporation project occurred during two periods that can be characterized as populist: an earlier one during the 1920s and a later one under Cárdenas in the 1930s. In 1917, despite the signals provided by the innovative, even path-breaking, constitution of that year, the populist direction was not yet clear. Indeed a division in the revolutionary family increasingly separated the accommodationist faction, represented by the supporters of Madero and Venustiano Carranza, from the populists, who sought to mobilize labor and peasant support. Starting in 1920 with the onset of the "Sonoran dynasty," the populists became dominant.* This period began more tentatively under the presidency of Alvaro Obregón from 1920 to 1924 and reached its climax in the following presidency of Plutarco Elías Calles from 1924 to 1928. During this period a state-labor alliance was established and the state came increasingly to depend on labor support. However, a party was not established which could perpetuate the state-labor alliance. This failure contributed to the breakup of the alliance during a conservative hiatus from 1928 to 1934 known as the Maximato, in which populism was largely abandoned. During the Maximato, however, the party that would ultimately perform this function was established. With the Cárdenas presidency, the state-labor-peasant alliance was reconstituted during a second episode of radical populism, and the party was reorganized to become the mechanism for institutionalizing that alliance.

Some salient features might be noted here about the Sonoran dynasty, the Maximato, and the Cárdenas presidency.

*The Sonoran dynasty refers to three Mexican leaders in the 1920s—Alvaro Obregón, Plutarco Elías Calles, and Adolfo de la Huerta—all of whom were from the northern state of Sonora.

SONORAN DYNASTY: 1920–01

The years 1910–17 had been characterized by political assassinations, rebellion, and civil war. At the end of the armed conflict, which had been bitterly fought and had taken a heavy toll in human life and economic and social disruption, the victorious Constitutionalists faced the enormous task of reconstituting the state and consolidating their power. In this setting of a lack of well-established central authority and fluid power relationships that were attendant upon the upheavals of the Revolution (as the whole period has come to be known), the creation of new political resources in the form of an organized popular sector proved decisive.

Yet prior to 1920, the populist direction was not well established. Carranza, the first post-revolutionary president, emphasized the importance of a broad coalition with economically dominant groups, rejecting mobilization of the popular sectors and alliance with them. The Sonorans (most notably Obregón and Calles) opposed this orientation and insisted on mass mobilization as the only way to consolidate the revolution. Obregón, who followed Carranza in the presidency, took a tentative step toward the mobilization of mass support generally and labor support in particular, but he adopted a basically conservative approach (partly dictated by the priority he gave to attaining U.S. recognition of the Mexican government) in which he played off all groups and parties against each other and refused to become dependent on any one of them. His presidency opened with what looked like a firm alliance with the dominant part of the labor movement. As presidential candidate, he signed a secret pact with the Confederación Regional Obrera Mexicana (CROM), the major labor confederation, which in exchange for a number of concessions agreed to support him politically and, for the purpose, established the Partido Laborista Mexicano (PLM) as its political arm. Nevertheless, the presidential term closed with labor very disappointed and substantial enmity and distrust between the CROM and Obregón.

It is with the Calles presidency that Mexico experienced a more consistent period of radical populism. Calles had begun to mobilize labor support early on. It was he who had made contact with the CROM on behalf of Obregón in 1920 to gain the confederation's support for Obregón's bid for the presidency, and it was he who, as

Carranza
Obregón
Calles

minister during both the Carranza and Obregón presidencies, did much to forge an alliance with labor. Furthermore, in the early 1920s rivalries among the Sonorans led to a narrowing of the support base for the presidency, as Obregón became identified with the agrarians, de la Huerta with the cooperativists, and Calles with labor. This splintering of the coalition meant that Calles came to the presidency dependent on labor as his main source of support. In 1923 de la Huerta staged a rebellion which challenged Calles's succession to the presidency, and it was perhaps the event that cemented Calles's reliance on labor. CROM took up arms and formed workers' militias in his defense, apparently playing a fairly decisive role in the outcome of the conflict (Carr 1976, vol. 1: 203). Barry Carr summarizes the degree of labor mobilization by Calles: "Never had there been a candidate, nor has there been one since, who devoted so much energy to cultivating the support of the organized labor movement" (1976, vol. 1: 209).

The concessions granted to labor in order to win and maintain its support are also clear. These consisted of unprecedented political influence at many levels of government, including the appointment of Luis Morones, head of the CROM, as minister of industry, commerce, and labor; material benefits, including both subsidies to the CROM and decisions by the conciliation and arbitration boards that were consistently favorable to workers; and significant state support for the CROM's efforts to establish hegemony over the labor movement. Again we can draw on Carr to summarize the situation: "All added up to a position of political strength unique in the history of Mexico and unequalled at the time elsewhere in Latin America" (1972: 13). In the exchange which formed the basis of the state-labor alliance, the government, in return for labor concessions, gained legitimacy and support. In addition, a potentially radical and oppositionist working class was converted into a cooperating labor movement that supported capitalist reconstruction and modernization—indeed one that pursued industrial peace and busted leftist and independent unions.

Typical of radical populism is the conservative reaction to which it gives rise. Despite a relative dearth of primary historical research, the argument can be made that as a result of opposition to the state-labor alliance and pro-labor policies, political polarization occurred as at least four major sources of opposition emerged.

Sources of oppstn

①   The first source of opposition consisted of U.S. interests and those in Mexico who favored accommodation with the United States. At issue here were the nationalistic petroleum and land laws which passed early in the Calles presidency. In this policy area, Morones was the leading proponent for the nationalist position, and his triumph led to a crisis with the United States and the opposition of the faction favoring conciliation. His political victory within the cabinet was represented by the resignation of Alberto Pani as minister of the treasury, the spokesman for the more liberal, conciliatory position.

②   The second source of opposition was national capital. Though the terms of the state-labor alliance led to the creation of a coopted union movement under an increasingly corrupt leadership that supported the government, promoted industrial peace, and rejected class conflict in favor of a collaborationist position, the shift in power that the alliance represented, the increased rate of unionization, and the pro-labor orientation of the conciliation and arbitration boards provoked the hostility and opposition of national capital. A study by Alex Saragoza (1988) emphasizes the primacy of the labor issue for the most important sector of Mexican capital, the elite of the northern city of Monterrey. Saragoza argues that for this group, "labor policy became the most visible point of contention" (p. 11). Furthermore, apprehension over labor policy and especially over the elevation of Morones to a position of such power and over the rising influence of the CROM was the most important factor in consolidating the Monterrey elite into an effective group that would defend its interests in the political arena (pp. 126, 129) and that would organize its political struggle on the national, not regional, level.

③   The third source of opposition was the agrarians, who were in conflict with labor over the issue of the organization of rural workers and were in competition for influence within the state as the indispensable source of popular support. As a result of the conflict, the Partido Nacional Agrarista (PNA) withdrew from parliamentary cooperation with the *laboristas* and announced its opposition to the Calles government.

④   The fourth source of opposition was the Church. The Church-state conflict had a long history in Mexico, and Calles entered his presidency with a reputation as an enemy of the Church, which in fact had taken a number of stands in opposition to the Sonoran vision of the Revolution. In addition to this background, the role of labor and the state-labor alliance may have been very great, and indeed even decisive, in the Church-state conflict that flared up during this period. Again basic research is scanty, but we do know that there was a history of Church opposition to secular unionism and attacks on the CROM, on the one hand, and, on the other, that the CROM and Morones had a leading role in launching and executing the state offensive against the Church, culminating in the famous decrees of 1926. Though it might be going too far to suggest that the attack on the Church was a political payoff for labor support, what seems clear is labor's central role in this offensive, resulting in Church opposition and the Cristero rebellion, which began in 1926.

Thus with respect to several issues, different groups were in opposition to the government over policies more or less directly related to the position of labor in the alliance. The Calles presidency seems to represent a case of radical populism in which the populist dynamic or contradiction discussed above is evident. The polarization inherent in radical populism led to a conservative reaction, which had a strong influence on politics in the following six years, before a more full-blown period of radical populism was initiated.

THE MAXIMATO, 1928–34

The following presidential term, known as the Maximato, was a conservative hiatus in which Calles held effective power, though not the presidency. The opposition and polarization provoked by radical populism was reinforced by the events surrounding the 1928 presidential elections, which further increased opposition to labor and weakened its position. In response to the controversial but popular candidacy of Obregón, Calles moved toward a more conservative position from which he accommodated Obregón and began to turn his back on labor. The coup de grace came with the assassination of president-elect Obregón. When the CROM was accused of being involved in the assassination, PLM members, including Morones, resigned their government posts and Calles named Emilio Portes Gil, an outspoken opponent of the CROM, as provisional president.

In the following years, the progressive policies that had characterized most of the Calles presidency were reversed:

> [Whereas] President Calles was anticlerical, prolabor, pro-pub-
> lic works, and nominally proagrarian . . . the governments of
> the *callista* period (1928–34) by and large dropped the anti-
> Church crusade, favored foreign capital, virtually abandoned
> progressive labor and agrarian programs, and sought a *rap-
> prochement* with the United States (Brandenburg 1964: 66).

The Maximato represents a conservative, non- or even anti-populist
interlude.

During the Maximato, a number of things occurred which are
important for the present discussion. First, Calles formed a political
party, the Partido Nacional Revolucionario (PNR), but coming as it
did in a pause in the course of radical populism, it failed to incorporate organized labor, which was not a part of the coalition embraced by the party. Second, a federal labor law was passed. Finally,
the labor movement underwent a major organizational transformation, and the state-labor alliance was largely severed before being
renewed under Cárdenas. With state support of the CROM largely
withdrawn, the labor movement underwent a process of disintegration as more and more groups withdrew from affiliation with the
corrupt and now discredited Morones confederation. The other side
of this disintegration was the resurgence of a new labor movement
that was more autonomous from the state and which, under the
leadership of Vicente Lombardo Toledano, was committed to autonomy.

The consolidation of the state continued to be a major concern.
No presidential succession had occurred peacefully and without
violence since the Revolution, and the assassination of Obregón
underscored the need for a mechanism to institutionalize executive
succession. At the end of 1928, in part in response to this need, Calles
moved to found the PNR. The new party served to centralize and
unite the still dispersed foci of power into a single organization.
Though in many ways the party was a confederation or coalition of
regional caudillos and revolutionary *caciques* (political bosses) and
their political parties and movements, it represented the first step
toward central political control. The PNR also served as the personal
vehicle for Calles, who was able to use it to maintain political power
without occupying the presidency. Indeed the party served Calles as
a mechanism of control over the president (Medín 1982: 40–41).

The hostility and opposition aroused by the Calles-CROM alliance virtually precluded the inclusion of that labor central into the new Calles coalition and hence into the new party (Medín 1982: 58), and the party failed to attract or incorporate popular support (Garrido 1984: 173). Neither the PLM of the laboristas nor the PNA of the agrarians, the two major parties with popular support, participated in the organizing conference of the PNR (Garrido 1984: 76). On the contrary, in 1930 these two parties joined other groups to form the Alianza Revolucionaria Nacional (ARN) in order to present opposition candidates in the congressional elections. Though a few labor groups did join the PNR, there was widespread hostility to it on the part of both the CROM and the major independent labor groups which during these years broke from the CROM (Garrido 1984: 116, 155; Anguiano 1975: 35; Dulles 1961: 518–19). During the Maximato, the CROM and the PLM remained in opposition to the PNR; the PNA, after it was brought to heel by the heavy hand of Calles's intervention in its leadership selection, subsequently joined the party.

Far from a continuation of the period of incorporation, then, the Maximato represented a rupture in the state-labor alliance. It was characterized by the abandonment of "*la política de masas*" (the politics of mass support mobilization) that accompanied the turn toward conservative policies, a change of direction which offered little to attract popular support.

A key aspect of labor policy was the passage of a federal labor law in 1931. Article 123 of the 1917 Constitution had defined a number of labor rights and paved the way for a federal law. The constitution was regarded as a triumph for labor, and a federal law that would regulate the constitutional provision was high on the labor agenda. Nevertheless, during labor's political ascendancy in the 1920s no federal labor law had been passed. The inaction of Morones on this issue was due to his uncertain ability to control the drafting of the law or to guide it in a way that would favor labor. In addition, Morones was ambivalent about a law that would limit his discretionary power to favor the CROM over other labor federations. Discussions of a labor law were held in 1925, 1926, and 1928, but, reflecting a political stalemate, they accomplished little (Saragoza 1988: 156). Finally in 1929, the first labor bill was introduced.

Labor, capital, and the state all had specific interests in a new labor law. Labor, of course, wanted a federal law that was at least as favorable as those already adopted in the states where labor was strong and had substantial political power. Employers were particularly eager to have a federal labor law. The diversity and confusion of a plethora of labor laws on the state level did not serve them well, and they saw a federal law as a means of achieving greater institutionalization of control, predictability, and uniformity in labor relations on a national scale. At least equally important, a labor law was seen by conservative businessmen as a vehicle to curb the power of Morones (Saragoza 1988: 135)—that is, an anti-populist device that would prevent a repetition of radical populism and the formation of a new state-labor alliance.

For the Calles faction a labor law was an important element in the broader policy of centralizing political power. Many governors and local caudillos owed their power to the patronage relationships they had established with labor at the state or local level. The Calles faction saw the labor law as a means of achieving central control, both over the labor movement and labor relations and over the political arena more generally, by depriving these local and regional political leaders of their power base. The law would extend federal government control over labor and make the federal government, more than the unions and their ability to strike bargains with local politicians, the source of labor benefits. President Portes Gil, the leader of the more progressive *rojo* faction within the PNR, introduced the bill in an attempt to gain labor support for the state in the post-CROM era (Saragoza 1988: 164; Medín 1982: 65). With this bill he sought to crush Morones's power and win the support of non-CROM labor. He saw in a new labor code the means to "outflank Morones, to undermine his support among workers, and to make the government—not the CROM—the key to labor's protection and welfare" (Saragoza 1988: 157).

In the end, the bill failed to pass because all sectors opposed it. In order to fit into Portes Gil's strategy, the new code had to be pro-labor even if it were anti-CROM. The CROM was aware of its intent, and independent labor was suspicious of the government's commitment (Saragoza 1988: 158; L. Meyer 1978: 151). Industrialists objected to the bill as "overwhelmingly tilted in favor of workers" (Saragoza 1988: 159) and more radical than the constitution itself (Córdova 1981: 52). The Monterrey industrial elite formed a national employers association, COPARMEX, to unite Mexican employers in opposition to the bill. Opposition also came from foreign capital, as both Henry Ford and U.S. Ambassador Dwight Morrow came out strongly against the bill. Calles's failure to throw his weight behind the bill assured its defeat (Saragoza 1988: 164).

In 1931, under President Pascual Ortiz Rubio, a new version of the labor bill was introduced that made more concessions to capital. Though these were not sufficient to win the employers' support, Calles's strong commitment to this new version was enough to ensure passage. The result was a federal labor law opposed by both labor and capital. Employers continued to object to the law as too favorable to labor. Nevertheless, labor found many of the provisions of the law deeply disappointing and detrimental to its interests. The law was more conservative than many of the existing labor laws and established practices at the state level. The adverse effects on labor were seen in the following months as a number of contracts were revised in favor of capital in accordance with the new law. Despite the opposition of both labor and capital, the law was passed by the Calles forces as a centralizing measure to consolidate political control (Clark 1973: 215ff., 228; Harker 1937: 95; Córdova 1981: 109, 113).

In addition to the founding of the PNR and the passage of the federal labor law, a change in labor organization occurred during the Maximato. The political crisis at the end of the Calles presidency served to discredit the CROM, and individual unions began to disaffiliate from the confederation. Internal discord within the confederation led to three important splits during the Maximato. In the first two, in 1929 and 1932, union groups abandoned the declining CROM and sought to reestablish a state-labor alliance for which the CROM could no longer be the vehicle. The third split, in 1933, was quite different and was the most important: it resulted from the disaffection of a reformist faction under the leadership of Lombardo Toledano.

Attracted to Marxism and close to the Comintern line and the Soviet Union (though not a member of the Communist Party), Lombardo became the major spokesman for a new kind of apolitical, non-collaborationist, class conscious, and militant unionism. Under his leadership a new labor confederation, the Confederación General de Obreros y Campesinos de México (CGOCM), was founded, and within a year it emerged as the strongest and most important labor confederation in Mexico, and the one, furthermore, that took the most independent, combative, and class conscious line (Córdova 1981: 204–8).

Thus during the Maximato the pattern of labor incorporation which had prevailed during the 1920s, and which was characterized by a strong state-labor alliance, fell apart. The unfolding of the political crisis led major actors in the state to abandon this alliance. With the decline of the CROM, no alternative confederation had yet emerged with which government leaders could form an alliance even if they wanted one. In reaction to the corruption of the CROM and the abuse of power associated with its alliance with the state, the new labor groups that were emerging adopted a policy of political autonomy and non-collaboration. Hence in addition to the disintegration of the labor movement attending the fall from power of the CROM, a parallel reconsolidation began of a new labor movement that had greater autonomy from the state and was more class conscious and combative. The CGOCM remained critical of the more progressive platform that was written by the newly emerging reformist faction in the PNR in connection with the 1934 elections. Indeed it declined to back Cárdenas as the reformist candidate in those elections. From the point of view of the state, therefore, the political integration of labor—the question of the way in which it would participate in the political arena—was again on the agenda.

THE CÁRDENAS PRESIDENCY, 1934–40

The height of Mexican populism and labor and peasant incorporation occurred during the *sexenio* of Lázaro Cárdenas from 1934 to 1940. This period displayed all the classical features of populism: popular mobilization and the formation of a labor-state alliance, concessions and reforms, political opposition and consequent polarization largely along class lines, and the formation of a multi-class party to channel and institutionalize the political participation of the popular sectors.

What was the Cárdenas project and why did he mobilize labor support? Cárdenas was not simply a progressive reformer, for he clearly had an agenda beyond the reformist program, as can be seen, for example, in the control that his government tried to exercise over the working class and peasantry, at whom the reforms were largely aimed. Nor was he simply a promoter of capitalist industrialization. In the context of our analysis, Cárdenas is seen first and foremost as a state-builder. His primary commitment was to strengthening the state and its political institutions (Hamilton 1982: 119), still fragile from the upheavals of the Revolution.

The Maximato had done little toward strengthening political institutions. During those years, a conservative policy orientation combined with the effects of the world depression had given rise to the heightened discontent of a rapidly changing and politically autonomous labor movement. In addition, the presidency was weakened by Calles's retention of real, behind-the-scene power. Though Calles is sometimes seen as an important post-revolutionary institutionalizer, establishing a government party and overseeing the first peaceful presidential succession since the Revolution, the order he imposed was in fact a personal one which left political institutions weak. The PNR became the vehicle for his personal control, which he exercised to the detriment of the presidency. During the Maximato, Cárdenas had opposed Calles's usurpation of presidential power and tried to bring about a reconciliation between Calles and President Ortiz Rubio to strengthen the presidency. Once elected, of course, Cárdenas had an immediate and personal interest in strengthening the presidency, since he did not want to fall victim to the Maximato pattern and become another ineffectual puppet president while Calles held the strings. In terms of state-building, the Cárdenas project can be seen as one of strengthening civilian political institutions, particularly the presidency and the party, against civilian caudillos like Calles and against the army, whose power was still not clearly subordinated to the state.

A populist coalition figured prominently in Cárdenas's goals. Popular-sector mobilization was the basis on which he could build support for himself and the presidency in order to establish independence from Calles. Wayne Cornelius's analysis (1973) has shown how few coalitional options Cárdenas had in confronting the Calles faction and how a populist coalition with radical labor and agrarians was the only viable strategy. This coalition also became a vehicle for building a counterweight to the army, when Cárdenas armed the peasants and formed workers' militias. Finally, with this social base of support the state was more able to establish autonomy from foreign and domestic capital and carry out the substantive reforms for which the Cárdenas period is known.

Cárdenas's mobilization of popular-sector support has been well documented and need not be discussed at length. Briefly, he offered gains and benefits that were ideological, political, organizational, and material. Cárdenas championed the cause of urban and rural workers and committed the state to intervene in the class struggle on behalf of the working class; he strengthened working-class organizations to defend their interests and encouraged workers to strike and demand wage increases; state arbitration decisions consistently favored labor versus capital; land distribution to peasants was increased and collective ownership of land was encouraged, as was the "socialization" of the means of production and the nationalization and introduction of worker control of firms unwilling to enter into fair collective bargains; workers came to occupy important political posts at all levels of government; peasants and workers were armed; socialist education was introduced into the schools; and the rhetoric of class struggle and Marxism was adopted.

The consummation of a state-labor alliance was dependent not only on the political strategy of Cárdenas, but also on the willingness of the labor movement to resume an active political role and renew its own strategy of collaboration with the government. Under the influence of the Marxist tendency, the labor movement initially had refused to respond to Cárdenas's overtures and to support him politically. During the months in which he campaigned for the presidency, Cárdenas established a new basis for state-labor relations and let it be known that his government would be sympathetic to labor, both in its efforts to organize and in its confrontations with capital. The immediate result was a significant rise in strikes. What should be emphasized here is the position of relative autonomy of the labor movement that Cárdenas initially encountered. Unlike the peasantry, which joined the Cárdenas coalition and actively supported and promoted his presidency, organized labor maintained its autonomy and stayed aloof from the electoral battle, though the Partido Comunista Mexicano (PCM), which was active in labor organizations, fielded an opposition candidate. Thus despite his championing of labor issues, Cárdenas was not initially successful in mobilizing labor support behind his candidacy or his presidency.

The coalition with labor began to be put together only in June 1935, when Calles, reflecting the alarm of the business community at the increase in strikes and the pro-labor decisions of the Federal Labor Board, used the occasion of a telephone and telegraph strike to criticize and threaten Cárdenas because of his pro-labor position. In the Calles-Cárdenas power struggle that ensued during the following year, the labor-Cárdenas alliance began to take form. Cárdenas, for his part, became increasingly dependent on the mobilization of labor support in the face of the establishment of a new party by Calles and of Calles's attempt to perpetrate a coup. Labor, for its part, was induced to support Cárdenas since the primacy of the labor issue in the Cárdenas-Calles conflict meant that the defense of the working class became one and the same as the defense of Cárdenas and his presidency. Thus was the populist coalition of the Cárdenas state and labor constituted.

Though the events of 1935 and the political dynamics of the Calles-Cárdenas conflict provided an obvious impetus to the political reorientation of labor, the change must also be seen in terms of the presence of different factions within organized labor, their particular orientations, and the effort to weld these factions into a unified labor movement.

The new united labor movement can be seen as abandoning its apolitical stance as a result of various factors. The first was the weakness of labor, which left it particularly vulnerable to an attack like that launched by Calles. Such a threat seemed willy-nilly to thrust labor into an active political role. In fact, in many ways it was the labor movement, at least as much as Cárdenas himself, which took the crucial and initiating role in precipitating the break with Calles and taking the lead in the power struggle as it shaped up during the final year, leading first to the temporary exile of Calles and then, in 1936, to the clear triumph of Cárdenas.

The weakness of the labor movement was in part a feature of the early stage of industrialization. The urban industrial work force was still small—indeed it has been suggested that it was smaller than it had been in the Porfirian era. Furthermore, perhaps half of the workers in manufacturing were artisans or worked in small shops (Hamilton 1982: 109, 112). As in the 1920s, many union leaders saw the support of the state and political connections as crucial. The new Confederación de Trabajadores Mexicanos (CTM) represented the reunification of labor into an organization whose dominant ideology was clearly Marxist; yet within this framework of unity, two distinct tendencies, already apparent in the Maximato, persisted. The first, based on relatively small, weak unions that were more dependent on state support, was the "pragmatic" tendency led by Fidel Velázquez and his leadership clique, known as the *cinco lobitos*. The second consisted of the stronger, more independent, and often more combative unions, particularly a number of important national industrial unions and unions in which the Communist Party had significant influence.

As secretary general of the CTM, it fell to Lombardo to mediate between these two tendencies. Lombardo was above all a firm believer in the importance of labor unity. The high priority he placed on it led him to capitulate to the Velázquez faction in crucial instances (Fuentes Díaz 1959: 338). In the interest of maintaining unity, the position of secretary of organization of the CTM was given to Velázquez. This was an important defeat for the Communist tendency, for the secretary of organization controlled procedures for the formation of both labor federations at the state level and national industrial unions. With this power, Velázquez took the opportunity to build up a union movement loyal to him (Hamilton 1982: 154–55). Thus the pragmatic tendency grew in strength as the Communist tendency became increasingly isolated within the CTM (Hernández Chávez 1979: 154).

As the cinco lobitos became increasingly influential, the CTM adopted a collaborationist position which enabled it to reap the advantages of influence, access, and official support that came with being an important, even indispensable, partner in the governing coalition. This coalitional logic must have seemed particularly compelling in a context in which the peasantry represented an alternative base of support. In the 1920s, Obregón had played the two groups off one against the other, ultimately relying primarily on the peasantry rather than on labor in a way that ultimately contributed to the dramatic collapse of the CROM. During the 1930s, the mobilization of both the peasantry and labor as support groups continued to limit the freedom of maneuver of labor; Robert K. Furtak (1974: 41), for instance, has argued that at the end of the Cárdenas presidency, the CTM supported the candidacy of Manuel Avila Camacho despite great initial opposition because of the threat of labor's being left out of the coalition and losing its political clout after the campesino sector declared its support.

As in the 1920s, a second factor behind labor's move to cooperate with Cárdenas was the weakness of the apolitical alternative. The stronger sectors of the working class, consisting of skilled workers often organized in national industrial unions, were less dependent on state support and political connections. These unions, however, tended to be under the influence of the popular front policy, which emphasized political coalition-building for the fight against fascism, though this position was seen as temporary and dependent upon the existence of a progressive government.

Against this background, the CTM from the very beginning began to move toward a political posture that supported the government, despite the anti-collaborationist position spelled out explicitly in the statutes of the confederation. At the CTM's founding congress, Lombardo had adopted the position that the confederation should support the progressive policies of the Cárdenas government and avoid political strikes that could weaken it (Hamilton 1982: 160-61). The support for the government became more unconditional after 1938 in the context of political polarization and the rise of conservative opposition to Cárdenas and his reform program (Hamilton 1982: 263). The CTM also supported the institutionalization of this support. In October 1936 the confederation responded to the PNR's initiative and decided to participate in congressional elections under the party's banner. Again, in the national and international context of 1938, CTM support of institutionalized collaboration was taken a step further, when both the CTM and the Communist Party supported the reorganization of the PNR as a coalition or popular front party with which the CTM would be formally affiliated (Alexander 1957: 338). Thus at a crucial moment, the apolitical, non-collaborative alternative was abandoned and, as we shall see, future attempts to revitalize it failed.

Even more than in the 1920s, the state-labor coalition, now in a more radical form, elicited tremendous opposition and political polarization. Cárdenas's alliance with the popular sectors entailed a political confrontation which "suggested that while the state continued to perform the functions of accumulation in the interests of the dominant class, it had abdicated its social control function and was in fact participating in the class struggle on behalf of the subordinate

class" (Hamilton 1982: 273–74). Strong opposition to Cárdenas's
policies was mounted on all sides, including the following: national
capital, largely led by, but not limited to, the powerful industrial
elite of Monterrey, which opposed the state-labor alliance in the
political sphere and the heightened level of class conflict in the
sphere of industrial relations and were "convinced that Cárdenas
was the harbinger of a socialistic regime where capital would be
slowly squeezed into submission by the state" (Saragoza 1988: 188);
foreign capital, which most forcefully opposed the dramatic nationalization of the petroleum industry in 1938; factions within the
military, which felt challenged by the formation of worker and
peasant militias as a counterweight to their coercive resources; the
middle classes, who turned increasingly hostile as they sought to
defend their position against the rise of the proletariat (Michaels
1966: 71); and the Church, which particularly opposed socialist education and the espousal of models of class conflict.

This opposition had many expressions. These included the
flight of capital abroad; attempts by the Church to mobilize opposition to government programs and undermine peasant, labor, and
student unions (North and Raby 1977: 46); an economic and diplo-
matic offensive by foreign capital that included an international
boycott of the nationalized petroleum industry; the emergence of a
rival mass movement, the *sinarquistas*, promoting conservative, religious values and opposing agrarian reform; the appearance of fascist
movements with connections to Nazi agents and members of the
Spanish Falange (Hamilton 1982: 261); the Cedillo military rebellion
of 1938; and the formation of a plethora of right-wing opposition
parties which ultimately coalesced, for the most part, around the
newly formed Partido Acción Nacional (PAN) and the promotion of
the presidential candidacy of Juan Andreu Almazán in 1940.

The result of radical populism under Cárdenas, then, was an
extraordinarily high level of political polarization. In a year-by-year
analysis of the period, Cornelius (1973: 440) concludes that the entire
Cárdenas presidency was a period of such intense polarization that
it should be characterized as one of crisis and confrontation. In this
context, and with the contemporary example of Spain a vivid re-
minder, the threat of civil war seemed real.

The labor issue was particularly salient in this polarization. It
was clearly at the center of the *callista* opposition, for it was over

this issue that the Calles-Cárdenas rupture broke into the open in 1935. Labor policy, particularly the initiative to form worker militias, was also a key issue in the growing distrust of military generals, as it was in the tension between foreign capital and the Cardenist state, seen most dramatically in the 1938 expropriation of the foreign oil companies. Finally, the labor issue was at the heart of the conflict between national capital and the Cardenists. It was the political alliance with labor and state intervention in the labor market, rather than any state policies to control capital directly, that was the source of political polarization and confrontation between national capital and the state throughout the Cárdenas period (Hamilton 1982: 215) and that accounts for the "apparent contradiction" that "a period of major confrontation between the government and the owning groups was a period of growth and prosperity for the private sector" (Hamilton 1982: 184).

The result was the intensification of opposition to the Cardenist state, the increasing strength and boldness of conservative sectors within the government and within the state coalition, and the weakening and retreat of the progressive Cardenist alliance. The beginning of the retreat from populism can be seen in the dramatic decline in 1938 of land distribution in the rural areas and of strikes in the urban areas, as well as in the choice of Avila Camacho, rather than of Cárdenas's progressive heir apparent Francisco Mújica, as the official party's candidate to succeed Cárdenas.

The final characteristic of radical populism is the incorporation of the mobilized popular sectors into a political party. We have seen how in the 1920s Calles failed to institutionalize his populist coalition in a party. The PNR did not incorporate organized labor, and a reorganization of the party to incorporate and channel popular political participation was a goal Cárdenas stated as early as the first year of his presidency. The reorganization of the PNR into the Partido de la Revolución Mexicana (PRM) in 1938 is the key event in the political incorporation of the popular sectors.

This reorganization had its roots in the early 1930s with the rise of a reformist faction which emerged in reaction to the conservative policies of the Maximato and which sought to revive the Sonoran orientation toward an alliance between the state and the popular sectors, premised on a reform program. That is, this faction sought to revitalize the political project of strengthening, institutionalizing, and legitimizing the state by securing popular support. The problem became one of changing the PNR from a personal vehicle of Calles to an institution which would support rather than oppose and weaken the state and the presidency. The institutionalization of mass support was pursued on two fronts simultaneously. First, there was an attempt to extend and strengthen working-class and peasant organizations. Second, Cárdenas sought to institutionalize his alliance with these popular-sector organizations through their formal incorporation into the party. The centerpiece of this attempt was the sectoral basis of party organization. Four sectors became the constituent components of the party, thus formally embodying the "revolutionary" alliance: the Labor Sector, the Peasant Sector, the Popular Sector, and the Military Sector (which was abolished in the next presidential term). Party membership was not individual but collective, based on membership in labor unions or organizations affiliated with one of the other sectors. Each sector was to retain autonomy and to serve as a channel of political recruitment and candidate selection.

This reorganization of the party was necessarily double-edged. On the one hand, it formally provided for labor representation and influence within the party. On the other hand, without a meaningful democratization of either the party or the unions, this system of labor representation was open to cooptation and control. A further limit on the power and influence of labor derived from the way the party's sectoral organization provided the state with a vehicle to structure the labor movement. By channeling their participation in different sectors, the party organizationally separated the working class, white-collar government employees, and the peasantry. In this way, it ensured the insulation of the various groups and allowed the state, through the party, to serve as the sole arbiter of inter-group relations, thus preventing a united, radical, and independent popular sector from emerging (Córdova 1976: 225; Anguiano 1975: 136; Garrido 1984: 250).

CONSERVATIVE REACTION IN THE AFTERMATH: 1940–52

The years following the incorporation period represent a direct reaction to the populist dynamic. The main characteristic at the end of the period of radical populism was a conservative reaction triggered by labor mobilization and progressive reforms and the sense of these more conservative sectors of being cut out of the governing coalition. This counter-reformist response demonstrated to party leaders the necessity of avoiding polarization and of formally or informally, but explicitly, including national capital and the middle sectors in a multi-class alliance. As a result, the aftermath of populism saw the establishment of new political structures—or the transformation of existing structures—to address the political crisis and instability of 1940. In order to retain power in the face of the conservative opposition, leaders of the PRM moved to the political center. In this way a major consequence of the dynamics of incorporation was ultimately the constitution of a new political center.

Radical populism, as we have seen, was not strongly anti-capitalist in orientation. Rather it was a reformist attempt by a faction of the political elite to consolidate political power and achieve some degree of state autonomy by mobilizing popular-sector support. Nevertheless, although the reforms took place within the context of state support for capitalist industrialization, the mobilization of the working class entailed more concessions than especially the strongest sectors of national capital were willing to grant. The concessions and reforms also alienated other groups whose interests were adversely affected, such as large landowners, whose land was expropriated, and the Church, which opposed the educational reforms and other measures which sought to decrease its influence in society. Opposition to the substantive program of reform was accompanied by the opposition of these groups to the form of politics—that is, an ascendant state-popular sector alliance that was embodied in a dominant and exclusive political party. The PNR/PRM stood virtually alone, with the exception of a few ephemeral groups during the period, and monopolized official political life.

Despite the opposition, the populist alliance was not destroyed, though it was considerably transformed as a result of the reaction of the political elite to counter-reform. The counter-reformist reaction pointed to the necessity, within this context of a capitalist state, of avoiding polarization, of including national capital and the middle sectors in the dominant political coalition, and thus of forging a new multi-class coalition, this time displaced to the right.

There were four components of this effort by the political elite to combat the conservative reaction in order to retain power. The

plcy chnges

first was programmatic. ⓣ The loyalty of the alienated dominant classes would be won with the adoption of many of their policy prescriptions—in short, with the substantial easing up on reforms and a policy turn to the right. The second was the exclusion of the ② left from the alliance. The third was the retention of the alliance with the labor movement (urban and rural) and the continued incorporation of labor as a support group. The fourth was institutional: the ④ creation of conflict-limiting mechanisms that would help avoid the polarization that had resulted in the threat to PRM dominance in 1940. The mechanism employed was the strengthening of the one-party dominant system.

These changes occurred during the presidencies of Avila Camacho and Miguel Alemán. The programmatic shift to the right to recapture the loyalty of the alienated economic sectors began immediately in the post-Cárdenas years and could even be detected in some policies toward the end of the Cárdenas presidency itself. On the most general level, the new policy represented a change in emphasis from social reform to industrial modernization. Industrialization became an increasingly explicit priority during the Avila Camacho period, and it was even more single-mindedly pursued by Alemán, with the new element of encouraging foreign investment. Even before this new economic model was put in place, however, the commitment to social reform and to the state alliance with the popular sectors at the expense of middle and upper classes was abandoned in favor of the new task of reincorporating the disaffected classes. Reassurances were given to the counter-reformist opposition and much of the Almazán program was adopted, so that a short time after the election, the Almazán opposition, which had been talking of armed revolt a few months earlier, announced it would be "Avila's best ally" (Hayes 1951: 101). The reordering of the coalition had a direct effect on labor policy and on state-labor relations. On the most fundamental level, the acceptance of class conflict and the need of the state to intervene on behalf of the weaker combatant, enunciated and substantially pursued under Cárdenas with his government's support of strikes and labor demands, was replaced by an emphasis on the promotion of class harmony and opposition to any special relationship or alliance between the state and labor.

The exclusion of the left from the dominant coalition can be seen most dramatically within the labor movement. Ex-president

Abelardo Rodríguez, a close political ally of Avila Camacho's, proposed a purge of the labor movement, and in 1941, under circumstances that remain unclear but apparently with government support, Lombardo was forced out of the position of secretary general of the CTM. With his departure, the Marxist orientation which had been dominant within the confederation was defeated (Miller 1966: 36).

The exclusion of the left intensified under Alemán when the Cold War replaced the popular front as the ideological context, and the labor movement split, with one faction maintaining a collaborationist stance and a more militant faction calling for independent unionism. These divisions were formalized by the organizational fractionalization of the labor movement. In 1947 a group of dissident unions abandoned the CTM to form the Confederación Unica de Trabajadores (CUT). The next year Lombardo founded a new progressive opposition party which became the Partido Popular Socialista (PPS). Another group of unions followed him out of the CTM and under his leadership founded the Unión General de Obreros y Campesinos de México (UGOCM). With the left eliminated from the CTM, the confederation assumed a strong anti-Communist stance and withdrew from the Confederación de Trabajadores de América Latina (CTAL), the left-leaning international, hemisphere-wide union confederation founded by Lombardo. Symbolic of these changes was the change in the slogan of the CTM from "For a classless society" to "For the emancipation of Mexico." The state-labor alliance, as embodied in the labor sector of the party, thereby also excluded the left.

Despite the reordering of the dominant alliance (the inclusion of the right and the exclusion of the left), the state-labor alliance was retained. Under the new leadership, organized labor continued to support the government, even though, in contrast to the populist period, the government no longer pursued a special relationship with labor, rejected class conflict in favor of class harmony, and no longer promoted unionization, strikes, or wage gains for workers— all of which stagnated or declined during this period. Initially this alliance, even under these conditions, continued in the context of the wartime popular front policy of international communism. After the war, however, many factions within the labor movement sought to resume a more militant, independent, and reformist stance. In this context of renewed labor militance, the state maintained its alliance with labor by means that were considerably more coercive—by the use of intervention in union leadership selection that came to be known as *charrismo*. The expulsion of the left and the coercive maintenance of the state-labor alliance meant that control of the CTM was consolidated by a collaborationist, entrenched, and self-perpetuating leadership clique and that the state-labor coalition became more asymmetrical, with greater union dependence on the state.

The final major change that occurred in the aftermath of radical populism—the establishment of new conflict-limiting mechanisms—was intended to avoid a repetition of the political polarization that marked the last years of Cárdenas's administration. Changes within both the PRM and the electoral system were made to strengthen one-party dominance. The former reinforced the shifts in the governing coalition and were aimed at decreasing the role of the party and subordinating it to the state, imposing greater discipline within the party, and reducing the power of the sectors within the party, especially labor. Particularly significant with respect to labor's influence were the changes that increased the weight of the so-called popular sector—that is, the middle classes—as a counterweight to the labor and peasant sectors. The membership in the popular sector was expanded to include small property owners, professionals, and small businessmen, as well as public employees, and the Confederación Nacional de Organizaciones Populares (CNOP) was formed as a new central for the popular sector to help displace the CTM's role as mobilizing agent for the party.

The changes culminated in the 1946 reorganization of the party and the transformation of the PRM into the PRI. Rather than the sectoral reorganization of the party in 1938, the changes represented by the reorganization of the party into the PRI appear extraordinarily important as the basis of political control and domination in Mexico. This transformation is well summed up by the change in party slogans from "For a workers' democracy" to "Democracy and social justice." With these changes, the power of the sectors was considerably weakened and greater control was lodged in the central party apparatus, as power was concentrated in the central organs of the party and greater hierarchy was imposed. In accordance with the provisions of a new electoral law passed earlier the same year, the PRI became based on individual rather than collective membership. The electoral and party activities of the sectors were restricted, and the system of nomination of party candidates was changed from the sectoral designation by caucus or executive order to one of nominating conventions and primaries.

The further subordination of the sectors and their organizations particularly affected labor, which had been the most autonomous of the sectors. Furthermore, labor depended on the power of sectoral organization to compensate for its relatively small numbers and geographical concentration (Scott 1964: 141). Labor was particularly vociferous in its opposition to the changes, and it was in this context that Lombardo left the party. In the following years, conflict and labor opposition escalated. Dissension was evident both outside of and within the party. In the face of these objections, the old system of sectoral nominations was reinstituted at a party convention in 1950, but only after the left had been expelled from the CTM and hence from the labor sector. Furthermore, the more hierarchical organization of the party was maintained, and the sectors came to comprise a system of support for the government subordinated to the central organizations of the party (González Casanova 1982: 62). In sum, these changes altered the balance of power within the party. Again slogans tell the story. Instead of referring to itself as a popular front organization or as a pact among the revolutionary sectors—as the PRM of Cárdenas had—the PRI began to make reference to a "political association of citizens" (González Casanova 1982: 59).

Another conflict-limiting measure was the 1946 electoral reform, which had the goals of avoiding a repetition of the opposition, polarization, and crisis of 1940; ensuring a decisive victory for Alemán; and using legal measures to ensure the dominance of the transformed PRI. The law laid out new requirements for the registration of political parties that had the aim of strengthening the government's ability to control the electoral process and the opposition by limiting the existence of small parties—especially local and regional parties, religious parties, and parties of the "extreme" left and right.

The one-party hegemonic regime that came to characterize contemporary Mexico must be understood with reference to the particular dynamic and contradiction of radical populism. Through the radical populism of the incorporation period, working-class and peasant loyalty was won through exchanges and concessions. However, radical populism also provoked a strong conservative reaction, which was responsible for a number of changes. The aftermath of incorporation built on the foundation of the state-labor alliance a new set of relationships between the state and society and transformed the intermediating political structures. The changes, embodied in the reorganization of the party into the PRI, altered the balance of power within the party by further subordinating the role of the popular sectors, particularly labor, which had been the most autonomous of them. The changes in electoral law institutionalized the PRI's preeminent position and the one-party dominant system. The expulsion of the left provided greater ideological homogeneity within the party at the same time that the PRI was able to construct and maintain a coalition of the whole. If the argument could be made that the PRM, as reorganized by Cárdenas, was a coalition party, at least by the time of the PRI reorganization it had clearly become a "corporative" party—a mechanism of interest intermediation which, as we shall see, was able to control its constituencies and provide a number of services for the state.

Chapter 3

THE LEGACY OF RADICAL POPULISM: THE MEXICAN REGIME AT MID-CENTURY

By the mid-twentieth century, Mexico had a well-institutional-ized one-party-dominant hegemonic regime based on a broad centrist coalition in which labor played a key legitimating role. In this role, labor provided the government with an important base of support which facilitated decision-making. During the period of radical pop-ulism the government had won the support of organized labor and brought it into the governing coalition. In response to the conserva-tive reaction that followed, the government altered and broadened the dominant coalition: labor, now without its left wing, continued to be included at the same time that the dominant economic sectors were brought in—at least in a programmatic way, if not in terms of functional representation within the party. In line with these changes and the process of conservatization that occurred, the balance within the state-labor alliance was tipped further from one in which organ-ized labor was a more or less autonomous alliance partner toward one in which labor was deprived for the most part of autonomous action but retained as a support group providing legitimacy for the regime. Though the rebalanced state-labor alliance, which remained at the center of the hegemonic regime, afforded the state substantial control over labor, it had to be maintained and continually repro-duced by an ongoing process of negotiation and conciliation. In order to maintain labor support for the government and its economic pol-icies—even when, at least in the short run, they were detrimental to the interests of workers—the government was obliged to engage in extensive cooptive activities and give at least some minimal level of protection to labor.

With this altered but still inclusionary coalition, a stable and hegemonic regime was consolidated based on a dominant party that virtually monopolized the political arena, allowing at best only marginal and largely symbolic opposition. This integrative regime contained the polarization, conflict, and stalemate that became a feature of politics in many other Latin American countries, and it had the political resources to defeat both opposition parties and dissident union movements.

OVERVIEW OF THE PARTY SYSTEM

Two features of the Mexican regime are of particular importance. The first is the nature of one-party dominance, which formed the basis of an inclusionary regime claiming to represent a coalition of the whole—or a coalition of the "revolutionary family." The second is the centrality of labor as a support base for the state and the formal, organizational links through the PRI which institutionalized the state-labor alliance and afforded the state a number of political resources.

ONE-PARTY DOMINANCE

Mexico emerged from the aftermath period with a hegemonic regime characterized by the overwhelming predominance of what can be called an official party. The party had not been formed out of either a parliamentary bloc or groups in society, but had been created by the Mexican executive (though this was originally the informal executive power of Calles during the Maximato) as an instrument for the centralization of state power. Accordingly, from the time of its formation and particularly after the changes of the 1940s, the party did not serve as a base of legislative power or as an organization for fighting competitive elections, but rather as a source of services for an increasingly centralized state with a weak legislature: it was a mechanism of executive power, interest intermediation for the state, and plebiscitary legitimation.

Though the dominance of the official party had been a prominent feature of the Mexican political landscape since the party's inception in 1929, its fundamentally unchallenged position was not attained for nearly three decades. The 1934 election had gone quite smoothly, but crisis reappeared around the 1940 succession. Steps were taken during the aftermath period to reduce political conflict through the further institutionalization of the one-party-dominant state, but this process was not completed until the following sexenio. Despite the changes in the electoral laws and the attempt to avert the opposition that crystallized around the elections of 1940, the presidential elections of 1946 and 1952 saw the greatest challenges to the official candidate since the party was founded. However, prior to the 1980s, these were the last "seriously" contested elections, and the one-party regime became well institutionalized thereafter.

The 1952 elections took place amid a sense of crisis that developed out of widespread disaffection caused by Alemán's policies. In addition to the conservative turn of his presidency, which alienated more progressively oriented groups, economic problems and blatant corruption adversely affected the sympathies of other groups. Furthermore, Alemán governed in a very authoritarian manner, imposing his will and running "roughshod" over the party in matters such as the nominations for governorships, instead of engaging in the traditional political consultations and negotiations (Brandenburg 1964: 103). On top of this, Alemán's attempt to impose a conservative successor over the opposition of other party leaders aggravated the sense of crisis and brought into the open splits within the revolutionary family and a clear emergence of Cardenist and Avila Camacho factions opposed to the Alemán faction.

Adolfo Ruiz Cortines, a compromise candidate with few ties to any of the factions, emerged as agreeable to all sectors, but the opposition generated by Alemán had not been overcome by the time of the 1952 elections. Opposing Ruiz Cortines was Miguel Henríquez Guzmán, who had been expelled from the PRI for premature campaigning for the party's nomination. With a background as a member of the Cardenist faction but with subsequent turns to the right, Henríquez appealed to many of the disaffected. In the election, 16 percent of the voters rallied to his candidacy, a level of support for an opposition party previously equaled or surpassed only twice in post-revolutionary Mexican history—in 1924, before the party was founded, and in 1946. With a small additional opposition vote cast for Lombardo of the PPS and for the PAN candidate, the vote for the PRI candidate reached its lowest ebb prior to the 1980s.

Up to the 1980s, the 1952 elections were the last in which the PRI confronted an unwanted electoral challenge. By the time of the 1958 elections, an economic upturn, a more even-handed performance by Ruiz Cortines, and a new electoral law further raising the requirements for party registration had all intervened to restore the official party's position of attracting 90 percent of the votes, despite an upsurge of rural unrest and land invasions and the onset of vigorous labor protest during the campaign period.

The 1958 elections constituted something of an inflection point in the evolution of the Mexican one-party-dominant system. Even more than in the vote tallies, the overwhelming victory of the official party was seen in the near disappearance of opposition candidates. The PAN as usual presented a candidate, but no other registered party did. Instead the two other parties backed the PRI candidate. The only other opposition votes were cast for candidates not formally registered, particularly a candidate of the Mexican Communist Party (Taylor 1960: 727). Having overcome its problem of consolidating electoral power, the PRI now faced another problem: keeping up the appearance of electoral competition in order to maintain a claim to democratic as well as revolutionary legitimacy. The government therefore turned its attention to the task of electoral reform to liberalize the requirements for party registration rather than tighten them.

At least as important as the problem of democratic legitimacy raised by the PRI's near electoral monopoly was the pressure to open the closed party system that came from a wave of protests and strikes in 1958–59. This form of political activity, which had not been channeled through the party system, opposed the regime's authoritarian nature and further challenged its legitimacy. Partly in response, in 1963 the government adopted an electoral law that for the first time increased the representation in the political system of the small opposition parties by distributing "party deputy" seats to parties that could not compete effectively in the single-member electoral districts. As we shall see, following the upheavals and protest that emanated from the 1968 student movement, the subsequent formation of many opposition groups, and the resulting new challenge to the PRI's legitimacy, additional laws were passed in 1972–73 and 1977 that pushed the liberalizing reforms of 1963 further.

Thus a key feature of the Mexican system was that it was a dominant-party system, not a one-party system. By the 1950s the PRI had come to rely on three minor parties to provide minimal or nominal electoral competition. The PAN was the oldest of these. It was also the strongest and provided the most consistent competition and outspoken opposition. Nevertheless, it was a weak party, incapable of winning more than a handful of seats in the Chamber of Deputies. Until 1982, it never attracted more than about 15–16 percent of the vote. Nor did it win either a Senate seat or a gubernatorial race, though it denounced the use of electoral fraud and over the years disputed the results of three of the gubernatorial contests (González Casanova 1982: 68–69; Levy and Szekely 1983: 70).

The other two parties resulted from splits in the PRI. The first was the PPS, formed by Lombardo at the end of the 1940s when he left the PRI, alienated by its turn to the right. The second, the Partido Auténtico de la Revolución Mexicana (PARM), was organized in the early 1950s by retired army generals. These two parties have often been seen as forming the "official" left and right respectively. Ideologically quite close to the PRI, they quickly established or reestablished cooperative relations with the parent party. Kenneth F. Johnson has referred to the former as "little more than the left wing of the PRI" and the latter as "a conservative extension of the PRI" (1978: 149–50). The PPS emphasis on a broad front in the service of anti-imperialism and on a reformist position advocating the development of state capitalism virtually mandated cooperation with the PRI. Advocating a more conservative position, the PARM nevertheless continued to accept the symbols and ideology of the Mexican Revolution and did not particularly differentiate itself ideologically from the PRI.

Neither the PPS nor the PARM could muster even the limited level of support attained by the PAN. In legislative elections they never garnered more than 3–4 percent of the vote, and in presidential and gubernatorial elections they almost always supported the PRI candidate. Only in 1952 did the PPS present a presidential candidate when Lombardo himself ran. In many ways, then, these parties could be considered satellite or electoral front parties rather than opposition parties.

The importance of these weak parties to the Mexican regime is underscored by the artificial means by which they were maintained and by the support they received from the state. This included public funds to support their activities (Levy and Szekely 1983: 76) and a bending of the electoral laws to ensure their continuing presence on the political scene. The minimum membership requirements for registration were bent to favor the PPS and the PARM, party deputyships in the federal Chamber of Deputies were allotted out of proportion to the vote won by these two parties, and all three parties were known to benefit from officially declared electoral victories that were not properly theirs, particularly at the municipal level. (Like the rest of the Mexican political system, electoral fraud was a complex institution.) The Mexican government clearly felt the need to sustain a weak opposition as a mechanism to maintain legitimation and channel political dissent (González Casanova 1982: 67–69).

Another party on the political scene was the PCM, which lost its registration at the end of the 1940s and did not regain it until 1978. Following its heyday in the Cárdenas years, the party experienced an enormous decline. It suffered under the impact of Communist strategy during World War II—including the policy of semi-liquidation in the mid-1940s—was rent by divisions which led to two episodes of purges and mass expulsions in 1943 and 1947, and had to withstand defections to Lombardo's new party, in addition to the government's Cold War hostility. Internally autocratic, having lost its way ideologically, and split into two (the PCM and the Partido Obrero Campesino de México—POCM), by 1960 the PCM had declined "to the point of vanishing" (Carr 1981: 13–20; 1985: 9). As we shall see, however, in the 1980s it took the initiative and served as the core of a unity movement among small left parties.

PARTY-UNION LINKS

Central to the hegemonic position, base of support, and political resources of the Mexican regime that emerged at mid-century was the state-labor alliance and its institutionalization through the close ties of organized labor with the PRI. From the time of the sectoral reorganization of the official party in 1938, the Mexican regime was characterized by formal organizational links between the PRI and the popular-sector unions of its mass constituencies among labor and the peasantry. These strong ties constituted a political resource which provided the regime with a vehicle for mobilizing support, controlling these constituencies through state influence in union leadership selection and activities and hence in the management of capital-labor relations, and achieving political stability.

At a minimum, party-union links mobilized support through collective membership in and identity of unions with the party. Beyond that, these links were the vehicle through which the regime could reinforce its legitimacy by making a show of formal endorsements by labor and peasant organizations and through which it could carry out political propaganda campaigns and organize mass demonstrations. The ability of labor organizations to fill the central plaza of Mexico City with workers and of peasant organizations to load their members into trucks to attend political rallies became well known.

Party-union links also were a vehicle of political control. The leadership of the Confederación Nacional Campesina (CNC), the peasant confederation, was particularly vulnerable to presidential manipulation, and the confederation often experienced a leadership change at the beginning of a new sexenio (L. Meyer 1976: 1303). A number of incidents also occurred in which labor leaders were imposed on unions by government tactics, the model for which was the *charrazo* in the railroad workers' union of 1948.* Though such incidents took place, these impositions and heavy-handedness were exceptions and represented the failure of "normal" mechanisms of leadership control. These included leadership cooptation that was available through union-party links. As members of the PRI, union leaders were in a position to be recruited to party roles, up to and including candidates for election to the federal legislature. With both appointed and electoral positions (the latter in a one-party-dominant regime being tantamount to appointment), the Mexican regime enjoyed extraordinarily extensive cooptive resources, estimated at about 43,000 positions to be filled as each new president assumed office (Brandenburg 1964: 157; Purcell 1978: 9-10; Johnson 1971: ch. 3). This vast system of leadership cooptation, enhanced by the distribution of material benefits other than political positions, was an important instrument of control not only of the leadership, but also, through the leaders, of the mass organizations and their grass-roots base.

The party-union links meant that the political and electoral activities of labor and peasant unions were channeled through the official party, where demands could be contained. Combined with the electoral dominance of the PRI and its continuing legitimacy among workers and peasants, these ties further eliminated any space for opposition parties that could claim support among the popular

*A charrazo is an episode of charrismo (see above). The pro-government, cooperative, or coopted leader who is selected is referred to as a *charro*.

sectors and present the challenge of more radical policy positions on their behalf. Within the party, policy positions of the mass organizations were moderated. The party had to triangulate among three different and often contradictory goals: support the state model of accumulation, maintain the state-labor and state-peasant alliance as a main underpinning of the legitimacy of the regime, and mediate the conflicting claims and demands of diverse social sectors. With the formal representation of mass organizations within the party, the PRI was a crucible in which competing demands were subjected to negotiation before compromise positions emerged in the public political arena.

The mass organizations did have influence within the party, but they were not able to initiate policy through their membership in the PRI: the party was not an important vehicle for the formulation of demands and aggregation of interests in a political system characterized by centralism and presidentialism. The role of the mass organizations was limited to influencing policy and modifying decisions (L. Meyer 1976: 1313, 1323). Most successful in this regard was the CTM, the largest component of the labor sector, which in turn was the strongest party sector; less influence was enjoyed by the peasant sector, the weakest and most dependent of the sectors. The main source of leverage for labor, which could be used only infrequently and in extreme circumstances, was the threat of breaking the party-union links—to take the mass confederation out of the PRI or otherwise threaten the state-labor alliance. More typically, however, negotiations proceeded within the framework of the alliance, and the popular-sector organizations were quite weak.

Party links were also used to transmit signals about what union bargaining positions the government would support, thus setting limits on union demands. In collective bargaining over wages, for instance, most negotiations took place at the plant level, but there were constraints on this process. Increasingly the guidelines for wage determination came to be established at a more centralized level in which the government played a key role. In the first place, the government as a major employer itself set wage policy in its agreements with the Federación de Sindicatos de Trabajadores al Servicio del Estado (FSTSE), the confederation of government workers. In addition, the government reached understandings and agreements with the CTM about wage policy (Zapata 1981: 364). Individual

unions thus came to know up to what point they could count on
political support and at what point they might encounter opposition,
from both the state and the CTM. This information was important to
unions, which, with some notable exceptions, tended to be economically weak and dependent on finding allies in their collective bargaining. In return, of course, they had to bring grass-roots demands
in line with the government position (Everett 1967: 165).

Control over the mass organizations was also enhanced by the
twofold pluralism of party-union ties. First, the mass organizations
were never unified organizationally but were divided among the
Labor, Peasant, and Popular Sectors of the PRI, the last of which
included several important unions of government workers, such as
the massive teachers union. This divide-and-rule strategy limited
horizontal ties among peasant, labor, and public-sector unions and
hence constrained their capacity for concerted action. Second, the
PRI admitted multiple confederations as members of the three sectors. Though the CTM and CNC were by far the most important
centrals among labor and the peasantry respectively, they were not
the only centrals represented within the organized sectors of the PRI.
With quite similar orientations, the various confederations nevertheless competed with one another for grass-roots membership. The
government thus had a mechanism for playing one confederation
off against another, as well as using an allied confederation as a
bulwark against a dissident union.

In addition, the party-union link provided a vehicle for dispens-
ing favors and resources. These concessions served simultaneously
as benefits and as a means of control. They were typically used to
maintain support among constituency groups when necessary to
meet any challenges from independent, more militant organizations,
thereby reducing the reliance on coercion. Quite apart from leadership cooptation, then, party-union links were a channel for organizational cooptation through which government-affiliated mass
organizations put dissident organizations at a serious disadvantage
as conduits for material and organizational benefits. The quid pro
quo for these benefits was playing according to the rules of the game
and maintaining the state-labor alliance on which the legitimacy of
the state was based.

Finally, these party-union links gave the government an unusual degree of decisional capacity even in policies that would result

in substantial belt-tightening on the part of workers—at least in the short run. The 1954 devaluation provides an example of the policy-making framework of conciliation in which the president could negotiate the support of organized labor.

The high-investment rapid-growth policy of the Alemán presidency of 1946–52 had been accompanied by high rates of inflation and balance of payments disequilibria which had taken the country into an inflation-devaluation cycle (Thompson 1979: 72–77). The peso had been devalued in 1948 and 1952, and another devaluation was undertaken in 1954. Though the policy was very unpopular in many sectors, particularly in labor circles, not only was it instituted, but also, with the cooperation of organized labor, a wage policy was negotiated which, along with other measures, was part of an economic package that ended the inflationary spiral and instituted a period of "stabilizing development" in which the Mexican government achieved price stability for the next two decades. Thus, unlike countries such as Argentina, Brazil, and Chile, where governments in a weak political position were unable to impose austerity measures as all groups fought to maintain income shares, the Mexican government had the political resources to orchestrate a coalition for a policy to achieve price stability and a sustained period of growth.

Despite organized labor's initial opposition, President Adolfo López Mateos had managed to line up a reluctant union movement behind the devaluation in April 1954. Particularly interesting was the less grudging support given by the Confederación Revolucionaria de Obreros y Campesinos (CROC), a new labor confederation that claimed greater independence from the government but that in fact had enjoyed government support. The May Plan settled on a 10 percent increase in wages to offset inflation. By the end of May, however, it became apparent that this increase was far lower than the rate of inflation, and both the CROM and the UGOCM of Lombardo rejected the wage policy. The CROC continued to support the president, but the CTM threatened to defect from the coalition. Under the pressure of grass-roots demands and a challenge for leadership within the labor movement (see below), Fidel Velázquez of the CTM moved into opposition, threatening a general strike and a return to "revolutionary unionism" in which the CTM would leave the PRI. Toward the end of June, the president undertook negotiations in which the government, employers, and labor worked out a modified interpretation of government wage policy that allowed a 24 percent wage increase (Everett 1967: 126–28).

During the following months labor protested and discontent was expressed, but the negotiated policy held. If the policy constituted a test of the labor leadership, the labor movement structure, and state-labor relations, that test was passed. In September a huge demonstration of workers was staged to support the government and renew the state-labor alliance. The stabilization policy was successfully implemented and was followed by a new economic model and a prolonged period of price stability (Pellicer and Reyna 1978: 94–105).

Indeed it was not until the mid-1970s that Mexico again experienced inflation and was confronted with the need for a stabilization policy. In response to the legitimacy crisis sparked off by the 1968 student protest and its repression and in the context of political ferment by opposition groups, the government of Luis Echeverría (1970–76) embarked on a program of "shared development" in which, compared to the model of stabilizing development, greater emphasis was put on issues of distribution and social welfare. With increases in social spending and an even more dramatic growth in the budget for economic projects (Newell and Rubio 1984: 136–37), public spending increased at the same time that attempts to raise taxes were effectively vetoed by the private sector. The resulting public-sector deficit led to mounting inflation, deficits in the international accounts, and capital flight, producing by 1975 an economic crisis that was aggravated by international inflation and recession. By the end of 1976 the Mexican government had reached an agreement with the IMF and embarked on a new three-year devaluation and stabilization program.

The outlines of negotiations and settlement with labor were similar to those of 1954. An agreement was reached through which a 20 percent emergency wage hike was granted to compensate for the expected price increase. During 1977 and 1978, labor leaders accepted lower gains than the inflation rate. In reaction, strikes rose to a fairly high level, but not as high as they had been at their peak in 1974. Furthermore, independent labor movements were not able to take advantage of this situation. However, by 1979, the final year of the program, this level of wage restraint was abandoned. As earlier, in exchange for symbolic and other non-wage concessions, a deal had been struck with labor on the implicit understanding that in the future material losses would be recuperated. Thus for a period that would be unimaginable in most South American countries, the Mexican government had the political resources to pursue a negotiated incomes policy that held the line on wages, and the "old-guard labour leadership . . . effectively rescued the regime" (Whitehead 1980: 854). The way in which, at least in the short run, symbolic payoffs could substitute for material gains and facilitate policies that imposed economic hardship was seen in the 1978 decision (hotly contested at the time) to formally redefine the PRI as a "workers' party" (*Latin America Political Report*, 18 August 1978, p. 255).

In Mexico, then, the political integration of labor gave the government substantial leeway to pursue unpopular policies, particularly in the short run. In this sense, the PRI was "a source of services which allow[ed] those in control of the state to make decisions and pursue policies" (Portes 1977: 194). Whereas party systems such as those in Brazil and Chile polarized decision-making, the inclusionary, integrative system of Mexico gave the government important resources for short-run "political management" (Whitehead 1980) and facilitated policy formation and implementation, despite the existence of opposition.

The PRI thus provided political, ideological, and organizational resources which allowed the state to maintain legitimacy, mobilize support, and control the organizations of the popular sectors. It is important to emphasize these mechanisms because they underline the fundamentally political nature of state-labor and state-peasant relations mediated for the most part by a hegemonic party. Though coercion and repression were certainly not unknown, control was primarily political.

We have argued here that state-labor relations were an outcome of the state-labor alliance formed during the period of incorporation and its aftermath, in which the balance of forces shifted further in favor of the state, the terms of discourse were limited with the expulsion of the left, and a reordered alliance was maintained. These changes in the aftermath period did not occur without some resort to coercion. This last point has received particular attention in many analyses of Mexico. It has often been said that what emerged was a charro model of state-controlled unionism based on coercion. Central to this model is the role of violence, corruption, and bossism, which perpetuate a nondemocratic, coopted, sometimes state-imposed union leadership that is not responsive to the grass roots but dependent upon the state and in league with it to control the working-class base and its demands in exchange for personal rewards. Such a description, however, is not complete, and it ignores the other foundations of what was a much more complex pattern of labor dynamics in Mexico. Specifically, it understates the fundamental need of the Mexican state to maintain the alliance with labor and the importance of the continuing exchanges between state and labor. Though altered, the initial populist bargain in which political support was exchanged for concessions was not superseded. Rather, it was in continual need of renewal, and the hegemonic resources acquired during the populist period gave the state the flexibility to make and withhold concessions as it deemed necessary.

Thus for Mexico a "dual dilemma" (see Collier and Collier 1991: 48–50) was constantly posed as a central dynamic of the hegemonic regime. From the point of view of the state, control over labor, social peace, and class harmony were desirable. Yet an overtly anti-labor policy was antithetical to the nature of the regime. Even the reliance for control of the working class on a coopted leadership which would be responsive to the state rather than to the workers and impose state policy over the working class could be problematic with respect to the hegemonic relation between the state and labor. Given the centrality of labor support, the logic of such a regime favors credible working-class representatives as union leaders in order to maximize its hegemonic controls and minimize its resort to coercive controls.

The union leadership was also torn in two directions. As José Woldenberg has argued, even a PRI-aligned union leadership required consent of the membership and legitimacy as the workers' agent. Since the leadership had only a limited capacity to act in a manner completely opposed to the immediate interests of the workers, the common position taken by the union bureaucracy was a broad reformism (Woldenberg 1980: 20). From this perspective, cooperation with the state was attractive not only as a channel of personal advancement, but also as a way for union leaders to seek institutional access and gain influence and concessions. At the same time, precisely the opposite relationship—autonomy from the state—could be a source of union power and bargaining strength vis-à-vis the state.

State-labor relations were thus complex, embedded in a complex political regime. As many analysts recognize, these relations were characterized by working-class representation as well as control through the union bureaucracy, and the mechanisms of control were primarily (though not exclusively) hegemonic rather than coercive, with the PRI playing an important role (Zapata 1981: 363, 384; Trejo Delarbre 1980: 129–30; Woldenberg 1980: 18–20). As Raúl Trejo Delarbre (1980: 130) has said, by the end of the 1970s a union bureaucracy in alliance with the state had maintained its hegemony of the labor movement over four decades, a feat which is inconceivable on the basis of coercion alone without the capacity to perform at least some representative function.

All this is not to say that the features of unionism depicted in the charro model did not exist in Mexico. They did, and the government did have a number of direct controls over the working class and unions. It did sometimes intervene and resort to coercive mechanisms. The corrupt, autocratic charro style of leadership did exist in some unions—and in some of the most important and visible ones. In addition, the government had the usual forms of direct control available through the labor law, such as the power to recognize unions, the power to declare the legal status of a strike, and a deciding voice on conciliation and arbitration boards and on the resolution of leadership disputes. There is no question that these more coercive mechanisms also played a role in the government's success in achieving substantial class harmony, holding down both strikes and wages, and minimizing the challenge of more militant, independent unions that sought a rupture in the party-labor alliance.

Yet the government had to be careful in using these forms of control. The political negotiations that underlay the coalition of the whole, which the Mexican regime embodied and had to constantly reproduce, required that the government present itself as a conciliator among classes by maintaining the appearance of neutrality between labor and capital; at the same time, it required that the government maintain the state-labor alliance (Camacho 1976: 502). The more general pattern of control and of state-labor relations, then, would have to be described as more multifaceted, embodying a form of unionism that had elements of representation *as well as* control—and in a certain dialectical sense, *qua* control. As this last point indicates, hegemonic and political controls were more pervasive and salient.

In sum, in Mexico the heritage of incorporation and its after-math was an integrative, hegemonic, one-party-dominant system which became an important conflict-limiting mechanism that avoided or minimized polarization. The popular sectors were electorally, ideologically, and functionally incorporated into the dominant party, which helped to mediate the relationship between them and the state. In all three arenas—electoral, symbolic, and organizational—the PRI provided the state with a number of important hegemonic resources. With these resources, the Mexican regime attained a level of stability that had completely eluded it through the first three decades of this century. As Lorenzo Meyer (1976: 1322, 1352) put it, the earlier open conflict of groups succumbed to the stronger forces of the coordination and conciliation of interests and the control of mass organizations through the dominant party.

Unlike cases such as Argentina, Brazil, and Chile, the Mexican party system, far from being a vehicle through which political conflict and polarization occurred, was an integrative mechanism and afforded the state substantial legitimacy. While electoral, symbolic, and organizational resources were unavailable to many other civilian regimes in Latin America, the Mexican state had the capacity to pursue anti-popular-sector policies on a short-term basis and to contain and coopt radical and independent movements. As we shall see below, the initial incorporation period did not tie the popular sectors to the state "once and for all." Rather, regular attempts were made to establish autonomous political movements and labor and peasant organizations. The point is that the incorporation period and its aftermath formed the parameters of the ongoing struggle, giving the state important resources with which to coopt such movements on a continuing basis and making opposition movements more difficult to mount.

DYNAMICS OF THE HEGEMONIC PARTY REGIME

The Mexican regime that was consolidated by the 1950s, with its dominant party and weak opposition parties, has been widely noted for its stability, but this was a dynamic stability in which the coalition that underlay the regime was continually reproduced through ongoing exchanges and in which the government displayed its widely recognized flexibility. The pattern of state bargaining that characterized Mexico has been referred to as "two carrots, then a stick" (Larissa Lomnitz, cited in Smith 1978: 57). Roberto Newell and Luis F. Rubio (1984: 121) have similarly identified three stages: first a process of conciliation and accommodation of opposing interests, followed by political and material cooptation, and, as a last resort if the first two stages failed, repression. This pattern of pervasive negotiation occurred both internally within the PRI and externally among the various parties.

Internally, the PRI embraced a large and diverse coalition through its sectoral organizations and geographically based electoral apparatus, party functionaries, and political bosses with their extensive clientele networks. In the inclusionary pattern of PRI politics, all of these interests had to be reconciled and, to the extent possible, accommodated in order to contain dissent. Cooptation was based on the expectation that political influence or material benefits would be forthcoming in return for political support (Anderson and Cockcroft 1972). The centrality to Mexican politics of negotiation and bargaining within the party was an important factor in preserving certain features of the one-party-dominant regime and impeding the course of democratic opening and reform. Sectoral organizations, especially labor groups, along with state governors and local and regional political bosses, were particularly resistant to even those reforms proposed by the party, lest a new political, electoral game replace the intra-party bargaining game at which they felt more confident of their strength (Middlebrook 1981: 18, 20).

For groups that remained outside of the PRI, another form of PRI-dominated coalition of the whole was created. In these cases ever more inclusive structures or higher levels of organization were established to incorporate the independent groups. This occurred in the party arena as well as in the arena of labor, as we shall see below. In the party sphere, the political reforms were an inclusionary device which granted minor opposition parties more legislative seats than they would otherwise have had. These reforms served to create a coalition of the whole not only within the party, but also among the parties—that is, within an integrative party system. In this way potentially anti-system parties were brought into the system. Becoming players in the established regime, these opposition parties in a minimal but nonetheless significant way thereby accepted it and had to turn much of their attention to electoral and parliamentary tasks and responsibilities.

The one-party-dominant regime of Mexico, then, had a number of political resources with which it was able to maintain a coalition of the whole through negotiation and accommodation. The dynamics of the reproduction of the regime can be seen clearly in the challenges presented to it by labor groups and political parties.

LABOR MOVEMENT

As we have seen, by the end of the aftermath period Mexico had a labor movement in which state-labor relations were mediated by the official party and, typically, by the close, formal integration of unions into the PRI. Though the stability of the Mexican regime—including the state-labor alliance put in place by the end of the aftermath period—has been emphasized in analyses of Mexican politics, underlying this stability was an organizational structure that was in flux and a series of attempts to replace the "officialist" unions under the leadership of a "labor bureaucracy" with labor organizations that were more autonomous and responsive to the grass roots. Challenges to this pattern of state-labor relations were almost continual in the 1950s and 1960s and reached a peak in the 1970s. The widely recognized stability of the Mexican system must be understood in terms of the constant renegotiation of the labor-state alliance. Given the political resources afforded the Mexican regime, however, these challenges ultimately failed to transform the system dramatically in the period prior to the 1980s.

Three types of challenges emerged within the labor movement. The first was presented by the CTM itself. It occurred at the time of the 1954 devaluation, when Fidel Velázquez threatened to take the CTM out of the PRI. Such challenges were rare and probably not much more than posturing: Velázquez and the CTM were essentially stalwart allies of the government and loyal members of the PRI. Nevertheless, the incident underscores the fact that the Mexican governing coalition was held together primarily by political negotiations—not by force—and that there was a limit beyond which the government could no longer retain labor within the coalition. Two features of the context of these negotiations taken together reveal the complexity of Mexican politics. On the one hand (as we have seen), beginning in the 1940s, the balance of forces shifted further against labor; on the other, Velázquez has been called the second most powerful man in Mexico. Lending indispensable legitimacy and support to the regime, as of 1980 Velázquez had retained leadership of the CTM for virtually four decades while a succession of the "most" powerful men in Mexican politics rotated in office every six years.

The second type of challenge consisted of the rejection of CTM leadership and the formation of rival confederations. Unity had never been achieved in Mexico, despite labor's long-standing goal to form a single central. In addition to the CROM and the Confederación General de Trabajadores (CGT), which predated the CTM, new confederations were formed in the 1940s and 1950s. This "pluralism" in the labor movement did not substantially facilitate labor autonomy or present much of a threat to the existing pattern of state-labor relations. Because of the advantages of access and the possible distribution of benefits that would ensue, virtually all of the confederations affiliated with the PRI. Instead of making state-labor relations more difficult to manage, the multiplicity of confederations allowed the state to some extent to play one confederation off against another, though the CTM remained the dominant labor player. One technique in dealing with the multiplicity of confederations was state support of umbrella organizations which would coordinate their activities but not displace them.

By the end of the 1940s, the labor movement was perhaps more divided than it had been since the Revolution. In addition to the CTM, several other confederations were embraced by the PRI: not only the CROM and CGT, but also the newer Confederación Proletaria Nacional (CPN), Confederación de Obreros y Campesinos de México (COCM), and Confederación Nacional de Trabajadores (CNT). Moreover, divisions had produced a dissident group within the labor movement that rejected PRI affiliation—specifically, the national industrial federations that formed the CUT and the group of unions that Lombardo took with him and that were affiliated with his new party. In 1952, in the last months of the Alemán presidency and with the support of the government, the CROC was formed by those that rejected CTM affiliation. However, the CROC joined the

PRI and added an interesting new element in state-labor relations. Because it embraced the newer confederations within the PRI (CPN, COCM, and CNT), it has been suggested that the CROC facilitated state control of labor by allowing the state to deal with fewer confederations (Pellicer and Reyna 1978: 74). The CROC was also effective in helping the government respond to the dissident unions that had left the PRI: a faction of the CUT opted to join the CROC, and the CROC's new secretary general was recruited from the ranks of the CUT. The inclusion of the CUT within the CROC and its consequent return to the PRI isolated the rest of the dissident labor movement. Two years later, most of the remaining CUT faction formed a new confederation which joined the PRI, and the Lombardists in the UGOCM were left alone and weakened.

The CROC performed another function which became particularly important under President Ruiz Cortines: it was used by the new president as an ally to counterbalance the CTM. Ruiz Cortines had come to power amid the discrediting of Alemán, whose administration had been both conservative and corrupt. As a compromise candidate, Ruiz Cortines had to steer a middle course between the Alemán and Cardenist factions, but in so doing, he had to restore the balance between the formerly ascendant Alemanists and the more aggrieved Cardenists—that is, he had to dislodge the former from their favored position. With the purge of the left that had taken place under Alemán, the CTM leaned toward the Alemanists. It has been suggested that Ruiz Cortines may have found competition and conflict within the labor movement a particularly attractive way to limit the power of the CTM, especially since the CTM opposed some of Ruiz Cortines's efforts to reorient policy; among other things, he sought a more balanced pattern of agricultural and industrial growth rather than the previous emphasis on industrialization (Scott 1964: 103, 164, 208).

In response to this attempt to support a rival confederation, Velázquez immediately began planning an initiative to consolidate the dominant position of the CTM. Manuel Camacho (1980: 54–55) has suggested that the CTM's general strike threat in 1954 over wage policy was part of the response to the CROC. Based on the principle of union "independence," the CROC had been projecting a more reformist, "authentic," and anti-charro image, despite the government support it received. However, with the threat of the general strike, the CTM countered this challenge and reaped the advantage of appearing more militant, especially when the CROC supported the government in opposition to the strike threat. In another move, the CTM took steps to unite the labor movement under its leadership. In 1953 the Plan de Guadalajara laid the basis for a united central, and in 1955 the Bloque de Unidad Obrera (BUO) was formed by the CTM, CROM, CGT, and several national industrial unions as a labor bloc to coordinate the activities of existing confederations but not absorb them. The CROC remained apart as a "dissident" confederation that rejected the CTM and the BUO. Nevertheless, the CTM retained its position as the most important interlocutor between the state and labor (Camacho 1980: 55).

A similar pattern was repeated at the beginning of the next presidential term. The transition between presidents saw a period of labor protest against low wages and unresponsive leadership (see below). Once again a new dissident movement emerged which rejected the existing labor movement structures, and once again the government needed a flexible response that would make room for labor groups unwilling to join the CTM or the BUO. In 1960 the government of López Mateos supported the formation of a new, anti-BUO umbrella organization, the Central Nacional de Trabajadores (CNT), that embraced the CROC, the electricians, and other labor groups that proclaimed the principle of independent unionism but nevertheless affiliated with the PRI (Reyna and Miquet 1976: 71–72). The final organizational capstone was put in place in 1966, when the Congreso de Trabajo (CT) was formed as a united central to replace both the BUO and CNT. Promoted by the PRI with the approval of President Gustavo Díaz Ordaz, the CT was dominated by the CTM, although like its predecessors it allowed its members a great deal of autonomy (Reyna and Miquet 1976: 75; Camacho 1980: 60).

The third type of challenge was the most significant. It consisted not only of a rejection of CTM leadership, but also of the pattern of "official" unionism put in place in many unions by the end of the aftermath period. From the beginning industrial unions had tended to organize nationally and furthermore to withdraw from the CTM. It was primarily from among these national industrial unions, often but not exclusively independent of the CTM, that "insurgencies" took place against a coopted and often corrupt union leadership and movements arose for union autonomy from the government. As a type of more militant unionism, this third challenge threatened to undermine control of labor demands, and as a type of autonomous unionism, it threatened to undermine the state-labor alliance which was a pillar of the Mexican regime.

The first major rejection of official unionism and the state-labor coalition occurred in 1958–59. Important strikes took place among the telegraph workers, kindergarten and elementary teachers, railroad workers, and oil workers, all of whom were public-sector employees organized in national unions. This wave of protest was a clear continuation of the struggles of the past and, in some cases, of the ongoing fight against the imposition of charro unionism of the 1940s. In each case wage demands led to a rejection of union leadership, which was seen as coopted, unrepresentative, and unwilling to defend the interests of workers. In addition to bread-and-butter issues, a major element in these strikes was clearly a rebellion against the coopted leadership and an attempt to supplant it with a democratically elected, independent leadership.

These cases of labor dissidence illustrate the characteristic flexibility with which the Mexican regime responded to the challenges it faced. The government granted a number of concessions, including wage increases, and even showed a willingness to abide by union elections and allow the dissidents to assume union leadership. However, independent unionism was not allowed to go so far as to threaten the PRI-labor alliance. If these concessions failed to achieve labor peace, the government intervened and once again imposed a nondemocratic leadership.

The state's response to the 1958–59 strike wave illustrates the mechanisms available for maintaining control in Mexico. In addition to substantive concessions, the state had political resources afforded to it by the hegemonic regime and the state-labor alliance it embodied. In the first instance, labor leaders within a local union or particular union section resisted the rise of a dissident leadership. At higher levels, the state found allies in labor leaders of the national union and then at the federation and confederation levels. At the highest level, the BUO entered the conflict on the side of government to oppose the insurgency against the union bureaucracy. In June 1958, for instance, the dissidents among the telegraph workers, teachers, and other groups rejected the FSTSE, of which their unions had all been a part, and attempted to create a rival confederation. In reaction, Velázquez threw the weight of the CTM behind the FSTSE and warned that he would mobilize the BUO "to crush any attempt at social disbandment against the regime" (Loyo Brambila and Pozas Horcasitas 1975: 40). The independent movements were repressed through the use of police or the arrest and jailing of leaders, but only after leaders refused the terms of cooptation, which exchanged concessions for cooperation with the PRI. Even after the government reasserted its control, the wage demands of the dissident unions were often met (Loyo Brambila and Pozas Horcasitas 1975; Everett 1967: 53–56; Handelman 1976: 271–79; Stevens 1974: ch. 4).

The 1960s were characterized by three developments. The first was a series of government concessions to labor. From the perspective of the government, the coercion used in the 1958–59 strikes reflected a failure of the smooth functioning of a hegemonic regime. In the following decade the government undertook to reestablish better relations with labor and renew the exchange of material benefits for support in order to keep labor in the coalition. Among other things, the government expanded social security and the system of retail outlets selling subsidized goods to workers, implemented the profit-sharing provision of the 1917 Constitution, and created a number of agencies and banks to promote the availability of working-class housing. In addition, the federal labor law was revised and the role of tripartite commissions was expanded (León and Xelhuantzi López 1985: 13–14).

The second development was the formation of the CT as the next step in the pattern of incorporating dissident labor groups through the creation of ever-broader umbrella organizations. As we have seen, the union bureaucracy had a parallel interest to that of the government in reestablishing control over the labor movement. To this end, the CT was created as an organization which did not carry the same political baggage as the CTM, even though the CTM remained the most influential component within it. On this basis, the CT could appeal to and embrace the CNT as well as the BUO and other labor groups. Despite CTM dominance of the CT, it has been argued that with the CT's formation the union bureaucracy not only consolidated its control but also achieved a greater degree of autonomy from the state (León and Xelhuantzi López 1985: 15).

(3)   The third feature of the 1960s was the continuation of movements for union autonomy. Though challenges were not mounted on the same scale as in the 1950s, workers in several unions met with some success—for instance, the unions of telegraph operators, petroleum workers, miners, radio station employees, and auto tire workers (Handelman 1979: 7). Nevertheless, the system was flexible enough to accommodate these rather isolated cases, and analysts such as Ilán Semo could declare that "in the decade of the 1960s charrismo established undisputed hegemony" (1982: 61).

All this changed rather abruptly in the highly charged atmosphere following the violent suppression of student protest in 1968. The student movement and the shocking and unexpected brutality of its repression led to politicization and radicalization. In the 1970s a new wave of labor protest centered around demands for union autonomy from the state and the PRI. The major sectors of the economy in particular experienced an explosion of labor insurgency, which was seen as a potential threat to the regime, especially given the other challenges to its legitimacy among the middle sectors, students, and private capital and given the possibilities of solidarity and coordination among different labor sectors. Unlike the cases of Brazil and pre-1970 Chile, where protest accelerated as part of a process of general political polarization, in Mexico, as in the 1958–59 wave of protest, the alliance of the dominant sectors of labor with the state gave the government the political resources to control and limit these movements. Pressure could be exerted against the insurgent movements, and an alliance with labor could be maintained after repression was used if that became necessary. Indeed by the end of the 1970s, this phase of labor protest had come to a halt.

In the late 1960s and early 1970s, workers in a number of unions successfully elected more militant leaders in sectors including autos and textiles (Handelman 1979: 7). However, the crest of the new wave of union dissidence began in 1972 in a context made more urgent by the faltering of Mexico's model of economic development. Following three decades of an "economic miracle," a growing economic crisis was reflected in indicators of GNP growth, balance of payments, declining rates of investment, renewed inflation (which had been held in check since 1955), and pressure on real wages (Ayala et al. 1980: 86–89). In this context labor protest erupted in unions both within and outside of the CTM. From mid-1973 to mid-1974 the number of labor conflicts submitted to conciliation and arbitration boards increased sixfold over the previous year, and in the following year the number of strikes under federal jurisdiction doubled (León and Xelhuantzi López 1985: 19–20). The most impressive movements were mounted by the auto workers, electricians, metallurgical workers, and telephone workers, as well as university workers, academics joining forces with blue- and white-collar workers.

The pattern of union insurgency was similar to that of 1958–59. Typically, the movement within each union started with economic demands and broadened as the existing union leadership came to be seen as an obstacle. In this way, the insurgency came to take on the dimensions of rejecting the existing union structure and advocating a more militant, representative, democratic, and autonomous form of unionism. Though the movement thus took on a political coloration—and indeed had profound political implications—it was not political in its origins, nor, with some exceptions, was it ideological or closely tied to opposition political parties, including the Communist Party, whose influence remained limited. To the extent the insurgent groups were political, they represented a diversity of views, and thus as a whole the independent union movement of the 1970s was politically heterogeneous.

This heterogeneity suggests another feature of the independent union movement: its fractionalization. Three groupings of independent unions are worth mentioning. The first was the Movimiento Sindical Revolucionario (MSR), founded in 1975 in the course of the insurgency among the electrical workers. Following a kind of charrazo in which the dissident leadership was expelled, the dissidents formed a number of organizations to mobilize support. Within the electrical workers union they formed the Tendencia Democrática, which was in some ways the most important single movement of the decade, promulgating a "Declaration of Guadalajara" which set the general agenda for independent unionism in Mexico (see Trejo Delarbre 1980: 140; Marván 1985: 36–38). On an inter-union level, the MSR was founded as a labor confederation that would constitute a socialist rival to the CTM (Handelman 1979: 8). In 1976, the Frente Nacional Acción Popular (FNAP) was organized as a political front that would coordinate worker, student, peasant, and popular movements. In 1976, however, the Tendencia Democrática was defeated; faced with widespread worker dismissals as a response to its strike activities, it disbanded. The FNAP never amounted to much. The MSR remained, drawing support primarily from nuclear workers and sectors of university and electrical workers. However, it never succeeded in becoming an important focus of union activity (see Handelman 1979: 9; Leal 1985: 62).

A second grouping that drew a lot of attention in the 1970s was the Frente Auténtico del Trabajo (FAT), which was Christian Democratic in orientation. It attained influence in dynamic industrial sectors, such as automobiles, electronics, and mining and metallurgy. By the end of the 1970s it had about 30,000 members. Finally, the Unidad Obrera Independiente (UOI) was the largest of the new groupings, claiming over a quarter of a million members at its peak but having about 50,000 to 100,000 by about 1980. It drew support from workers in automobile, chemical, and textile industries, as well as in the transportation sector. Its orientation was one of "militantly antipolitical economism" (Leal 1985: 66–67, 85; Carr 1983: 94, 95).

Compared to the 1958–59 strikes, the movement of the 1970s was characterized by a greater magnitude, both encompassing more sectors and lasting over a number of years. Furthermore, it presented a greater challenge, with the possibility of coordinated action among different working-class sectors and solidarity movements with students and the new left parties, particularly in the context of more general political ferment and of the regime's more fragile legitimacy. Nevertheless, the wave of protest was overcome with the same combination of responses, in which the government relied on its legal powers to recognize unions (and to decline recognition) and decide on the legality of strikes; on the presence of a labor bureaucracy through which it could funnel benefits to workers and recruit an alternative, cooperative leadership; and on coercive means when a more flexible response failed to secure cooperation.

By the end of the Echeverría government in 1976, the labor challenge to the regime had been overcome. The CTM was not dislodged from its dominant position, and the CT continued to encompass most of organized labor. In the mid-1970s, three quarters of the estimated CT members were affiliated with one of the "official" confederations. Of these, almost half, or nearly 1.5 million workers, belonged to the CTM, representing a greater percentage than membership data indicate for 1948, 1954, and 1960. Labor organizations that rejected affiliation with the four-million-strong CT were a small percentage of the labor movement. At the end of the decade the UOI numbered about 106,000, the FAT about 30,000, and another organization (Sindicato de Obreros Libres—SOL), about 7,000. Adding the higher estimates available for three unaffiliated national industrial unions (for university workers, aircraft workers, and aviation workers) brings the total number of independent workers to, at most, under 200,000—or about 4 percent of the organized work force (Leal 1985: 39–40, 67–68, 85; Aguilar García 1985: 205–9).

Emphasizing the "durability of officially-sanctioned unionism," Carr has seen the 1970s as "a history of the enormous resilience of the 'official' labor union leadership and an illustration of the difficulties facing independent unions . . . which would threaten the existing pattern of relations between the state and the labor bureaucracy" (1983: 92–93, 96). Yet as he recognizes, the defeat did not represent a complete failure. Though the CT continued to be the dominant interlocutor of the labor movement, Samuel León and María Xelhuantzi López (1985: 26) have emphasized the way it was transformed by the dynamics within the labor movement and the way it came to put greater emphasis on consensus and representation instead of coercion and violence. With the defeat of the dissident movement of the 1970s, the struggle was largely displaced to the transformation of existing organizations within established channels (Trejo Delarbre 1980: 151).

In sum, Mexican unions were under strong pressure to participate in the state-labor coalition. The economic weakness of most unions and their need to find allies in collective bargaining made them particularly vulnerable to this pressure (Everett 1967: 165). When dissident movements emerged among the economically stronger unions, the government was flexible and willing to tolerate substantial independence, but only within the framework of sustaining the overall PRI-labor alliance (Handelman 1976: 289). In cases of intransigent opposition, the government had both hegemonic and coercive resources to defeat the dissident movements and maintain the coalition.

POLITICAL PARTIES AND ELECTORAL REFORM

In the party sphere, as we have seen, the presence of the PPS, the PARM, and the PAN failed to constitute a major challenge to the one-party-dominant regime as Mexico emerged from the aftermath period. Quite the contrary, the existence of these parties could be said to have contributed to the smooth functioning of the regime by providing a loyal opposition of weak parties. Nor did the Communist Party present any real challenge: "By 1957 the PCM's feeble membership, organizational chaos, and leadership style had almost succeeded in destroying the party as a real political force" (Carr 1985: 11). The Mexican regime was not, however, immune from the challenges of radicalization and the formation of new opposition parties in the 1960s and 1970s. The challenges of the 1960s were contained through the usual mechanisms and hegemonic resources available to the regime; the implications of a second round of political mobilization and opposition which occurred in the 1970s in the wake of the 1968 student movement were still being worked out as the 1980s began.

In the 1960s, a political reorientation was stimulated by the Cuban Revolution, which provided the fragmented Mexican left with a new revolutionary model and stimulated renewed militancy, a new organizational drive, and a common focus of attention. At a pro-Cuban international conference held in March 1961, the Mexican delegation determined to unite in the Movimiento de Liberación Nacional (MLN), a form of left front organization that was being encouraged by the Soviet Union at the time. The following month, a diverse group of the Mexican left—including Lombardo and the PPS, the PCM, and Lázaro Cárdenas and his supporters—agreed on a common political position which denounced the PRI's betrayal of the Mexican Revolution and called for its revitalization in a program that included agrarian reform, autonomy of trade unions and peasant collectives (*ejidos*), Mexican control of natural resources, nationalization of certain industries, just division of national wealth, the freeing of political prisoners, solidarity with Cuba, and opposition to U.S. imperialism. In terms of tactics, the MLN followed the Cuban example and emphasized the role of the peasantry, advocating its organization into a militant revolutionary force (Garza 1964: 450, 454).

In 1963, a new electoral reform made it easier for parties to win seats in the Chamber of Deputies: through a type of proportional representation, additional seats for "party deputies" were allocated to minority parties able to capture at least 2.5 percent of the national vote. The goal of the reform was to channel the political conflict that had erupted in the 1958–59 strikes and to mitigate the opposition that was emerging at the close of the 1950s, inspired by the Cuban Revolution (Middlebrook 1981: 11). Responding to this incentive, the MLN formed the Frente Electoral Popular (FEP) as an electoral front to contest the elections. The FEP, however, failed to demonstrate enough support to even qualify for registration. Nevertheless, it illegally entered a candidate and took the occasion of the campaign to attack the PRI and advocate political violence. After the election, its candidate was arrested, and both the MLN and the FEP petered out (Johnson 1971: 116).

In the end, the MLN and the FEP failed to achieve any success for perhaps two reasons. First, in a context in which the PRI had overwhelming popular support, there was little room for the successful mobilization of grass-roots support. Second, the one-party-dominant system, which incorporated the PPS as a loyal opposition party, intensified and perpetuated the fragmentation of the left, thereby contributing to its weakness. Less than a year after the MLN was formed, Lombardo withdrew the PPS, arguing the advantages of loyal opposition and support for the "national bourgeoisie and State capitalism as an anti-imperialistic formula" (cited in Garza 1964: 452) and the inappropriateness of a mechanically borrowed Cuban model. The MLN, in turn, responded with ideological attacks on Lombardo's "peaceful transition to power through legal means" and championed forms of direct action and agitation (Garza 1964: 452–53). Such splits were debilitating for the left. Ultimately the diffusion of post-Castro radicalization never amounted to much in the Mexican hegemonic context.

As noted, as fallout of the 1968 student protests and their repression, a new round of political organizing and opposition occurred. The legitimacy of the regime had been particularly threatened by the inability to hold the inclusionary coalition together without resort to violent repression, and the repression had had the effect of radicalizing Mexican intellectuals, leading to their widespread disaffection. Labor and middle-class groups had also reacted. In response to the political ferment, the Echeverría government once again moved to incorporate and channel dissident groups into a legally defined and delimited electoral arena. Partly under this impetus, but also as an expression of autonomous oppositional ferment, a number of new parties were organized, primarily but not exclusively to oppose the PRI from the left.

Echeverría undertook to integrate dissident groups through substantive policies and a democratic opening to the left that would attract and coopt them. His initiatives included a populist rhetoric that emphasized solidarity with the Third World and championed social justice both internationally and domestically. The rhetoric was backed up by policies that distributed material benefits to key groups: wage increases, price controls on basic commodities, expansion of student scholarships, and additional public investment and credit in rural areas, where land invasions were also tolerated to some extent. In addition, Echeverría attempted a fiscal reform, but capitalists were successful in scuttling it and preserving their low-tax position. Finally, he introduced greater press freedom and released some of the political prisoners from the 1968 student movement.

In addition to these measures, Echeverría introduced a series of electoral reforms. Motivated by the same need to handle dissidence as the 1963 reforms, these built on the earlier attempt to expand the participation and representation of minority parties. A 1972 reform lowered the minimum national vote required for a party to be awarded a party deputy from 2.5 to 1.5 percent, while the maximum number of party deputies was increased from twenty to twenty-five. Another reform the following year reduced the minimum membership required by a party for legal registration. Finally, in 1975 the PRI published a statement outlining the direction of future reforms. These were not acted upon during the Echeverría presidency, but their author had a decisive role in the reforms that were adopted early in the next presidential term (Middlebrook 1981: 11, 13).

Also in the 1970s, new parties appeared on the scene, representing both a burst of organizational creativity and change, as well as a process of fragmentation on the left. In 1971 groups from the dissident railroad workers movement of 1958–59, the MLN, and the 1968 student movement combined to form the Comité Nacional de Auscultación y Coordinación (CNAC). The unity did not last long, however, and by 1976 the CNAC had splintered into several separate and competing parties. Of these, three would retain some electoral importance and organizational identity: the Partido Mexicano de Trabajadores (PMT), which had connections with some of the most important dissident groups in the labor movement; the Partido Socialista de los Trabajadores (PST), which grew close to Echeverría and the left of the PRI; and the Partido Socialista Revolucionario (PSR). In addition, in 1977 the Partido del Pueblo Mexicano (PPM) split from the PPS. On the two ends of the ideological spectrum, the Partido Revolucionario de los Trabajadores (PRT) emerged as a Trotskyist party, and on the right, the Partido Demócrata Mexicano (PDM) was formed as the electoral arm of the organizational descendants of the sinarquistas (Rodríguez Araujo 1982).

By the time the new president, José López Portillo, took office in 1976, the urgency for further reform had become acute. The economic crisis was accompanied by a political crisis as opposition to the overall reformist tilt of the outgoing president was aggravated by a set of highly visible and contentious expropriations in response to peasant land invasions in the last months of Echeverría's term. The right was alarmed, and none of the new parties had yet been channeled into the legal electoral arena: despite the liberalized law, no additional parties, including the Communist Party, had enough support to meet the legal requirements for registration and hence could not compete in the 1976 elections, no less become eligible for party deputies. To make matters worse, from the point of view of the regime, far from encompassing more opposition parties, the 1976 presidential elections had not even had the usual advantage of minimal competition from the PAN. Due to internal disputes, that party had not been able to nominate a presidential candidate, and the facade of competitive democracy was brought down, as the PPS and the PARM, the only other nominal opposition parties, continued their pattern of supporting the PRI candidate.

High on the agenda of the new president, therefore, was renewed attention to the problem of electoral reform, which was enacted at the end of the first year of López Portillo's term. Again, the requirements for legal registration were substantially lowered, though, as Kevin Middlebrook (1981: 24) points out, they were not eliminated and the state retained important controls on the entry of parties into the electoral arena. The idea of party deputies was expanded by a more fundamental reform of the Chamber of Deputies, which was enlarged to 400, one-fourth of which would not be elected in majority districts like the others but would be reserved for minority party delegates elected by proportional representation.

Other measures aimed at reducing electoral fraud and expanding opposition party access to mass media.

It was important to the government to show some quick results by the 1979 mid-term elections. Specifically, the government wanted at a minimum to achieve the formal participation of the PCM, PDM, PST,and PMT, the first two representing opposite ends of the ideological spectrum and the last two representing left-of-center coalitions. These were the largest and most important of the unregistered parties (Middlebrook 1981: 17).

The unregistered parties energetically debated whether or not to participate in electoral politics. They were presented with the same dilemma that we have discussed with respect to labor. On the one hand, the electoral arena offered an opportunity to mobilize support and at the very least to advance a national platform in a highly visible campaign. With some degree of electoral success, there was even the possibility of having some influence on policy-making in the Chamber of Deputies. On the other hand, there was a possibility of cooptation by participation in the electoral arena and the compromise of substantive goals through the logic of electoral mobilization. Despite differences in political outlook and orientation, almost all parties resolved this dilemma in favor of registration, with the major exception of the PMT. Of the others, only the PCM, PDM, and PST qualified for registration for the 1979 elections.

Not only did more parties participate, but also necessarily according to the new rules, their representation in the Chamber of Deputies increased from 17.4 percent under the party deputy system in effect in 1976 to 26 percent in 1979—just one percent more than was reserved for the opposition in the proportional representation seats (representing a PAN victory of four majority seats). In these elections, in which the incidence of electoral fraud was apparently reduced, the PRI vote declined—to "only" 70 percent. In relatively clean elections, then, the popularity of the PRI remained strong (Levy and Szekely 1983: 68–70; Baer and Bailey 1985: 5).

A second reform project, the reform of the PRI itself, was much less successful in the period before 1980 in the sense that despite repeated attempts it was never implemented, except in a very partial and temporary way. This reform was aimed at opening the party to greater grass-roots participation and introducing internal democratic procedures that could replace control by party bosses. This was not

the first time projects to democratize the party had been adopted—
nor indeed the first time they had failed. The first attempt, in 1946,
has been mentioned above. That experience is particularly instruc-
tive in highlighting the contradictory nature of such a reform. The
1946 reforms took place during the height of the conservative reaction to radical populism and in a context of a new pro-business
economic policy that emphasized rapid growth and industrialization. These internal dynamics were reinforced internationally by the
onset of the Cold War, which ushered in an anti-labor period. The
dynamics of the 1946 attempt, which was defeated primarily because
of labor opposition, underscore the way in which the introduction
of party primaries and a process of internal democratization is
consistent with an anti-labor orientation—i.e., with a policy of labor
demobilization and subordination within the coalition.

Another party reform project was instituted at the end of 1964,
when President Díaz Ordaz appointed Carlos Madrazo as president
of the PRI's National Executive Committee to revitalize the party at
the grass roots, attack corruption and bossism within the party,
reinvigorate the party as an organization separate from the government, and produce more attractive leaders and candidates. The
mechanism to begin this task was the introduction of internal party
primaries for municipal elections. These primaries, however, came
into direct conflict with state governors, who exercised considerable
control over municipal elections. In the battle that ensued, those who
opposed reform proved more powerful, and by 1965 the project was
abandoned (Bailey 1988: 109–10).

The effort to achieve internal party reform was renewed in the
1970s, as yet another initiative was undertaken during each succes-
sive sexenio. The first occurred under President Echeverría and the
party leadership of Jesús Reyes Heroles, who argued for the need to
improve the quality of PRI candidates—a change that would be
particularly important with the anticipated electoral law of 1977. Yet
another reform was introduced in 1977–78 under President López
Portillo and the party leadership of Carlos Sansores Pérez, who
sponsored a project of "transparent democracy." This was in conception a more pliable reform in which various nominating procedures,
including primaries, party assemblies, and auscultation,* would be

*Auscultation was to be a procedure of choosing among potential candidates
by "listening" to their positions.

employed in different places. In the beginning of 1979, however, this reform too was abandoned under pressure from traditional political interests within the party (Bailey 1988: 112, 114).

All in all, the one-party hegemonic regime in Mexico had remarkable staying power. It had substantial political resources to reproduce and sustain itself through a process of flexible adjustment, based on constant negotiation and conciliation, substantial cooptive capacity, and occasional reforms of the electoral system and (less successfully) of the PRI itself. Especially in the wake of 1968, the regime faced a considerable challenge with respect to both labor dissidence and party opposition, but it seemed to have the political resources to overcome it. During this same period and under similar economic and political pressures civilian regimes throughout Latin America fell to military coups in the face of polarization and opposition, but the dynamics of the Mexican regime seemed to tend toward reequilibration rather than mounting tensions and crisis, and the Mexican regime remained stable in the face of the political and economic challenges.

Chapter 4

POLITICAL REORIENTATION IN THE 1980s: POLITICS UNDER DE LA MADRID

The legacy of radical populism was ultimately a hegemonic party regime that provided stability, legitimacy, and impressive decision-making capacity, largely through party links with mass popular-sector organizations. Against this background, how does one interpret the startling success of the opposition in the 1988 national elections? On that occasion, discontent burst forth in the dramatic success of Cuauhtémoc Cárdenas, son of the former president, who broke with the PRI to stand as an opposition candidate on a platform of democratization, nationalism, and a reorientation of policy toward a reformism that would address the forgotten issues of social justice and equitable development. The electoral outcome, clearly marked by fraud, was highly contested, with Cárdenas claiming victory. Even in the official results, the PRI was reduced to just half of the votes, an outcome that seemed to mark the onset of a new political era. Do the events of 1988 represent another, albeit more dramatic and more significant, in a series of challenges to the regime which have in the past been met and overcome? Or do they represent a fundamental shift in Mexican politics—the end of the one-party-dominant regime and/or of the underlying coalition on which it was based?

The changes in the Mexican regime can be assessed in light of three possibilities. The key factors to consider are the underlying organization of politics, the social base of the state, the pattern of political alliances and cleavages, and how these are institutionalized in the party system. First, there may be a change in the party system—but one that does not amount to a significant change of regime. For instance, opposition parties may become more important. Change may thus take place at the formal, structural level of the electoral law and of the party system, as opposition parties may

71

72	*Ruth Berins Collier*

come to win greater representation and the regime may become more competitive. Nevertheless, this may be compatible with little change in terms of the hegemonic regime characterized by the leading role of the PRI, the inclusionary coalition, and the same underlying base of support. In other words, some change may take place, but of a type that should be interpreted as essentially a reproduction of the Mexican regime.

(2) Second, no real change may occur in the party system—for instance, the opposition may falter and retreat—but change may occur in the social base of the state and in the lines of political cleavage and coalitions. This is a pattern noted by analysts of critical elections in the United States and by some observers of advanced capitalist countries in trying to assess the impact of the rise of new "post-material" issues. In this pattern one would see continuity in political structures—for instance, in constitutional arrangements and in the party system. Little innovation would take place in terms of the creation of new parties or the changing importance of old ones, and no fundamental modification would occur in the party system. However, in this pattern the old parties are viewed as vessels that become filled with new contents—new wine in old bottles. Hence, though the party system remains remarkably stable, the coalitional or sectoral basis of the parties and of politics more generally may change fundamentally.

(3) Third, one may see a change in both the underlying political coalitions and the party system. In other words, in this case the changes described in the second alternative are accompanied by changes in political structures. However, these latter changes are not slight alterations, as would occur in the first case, but rather are more basic. The coalitional changes are institutionalized in new party structures, and the political dynamics of the regime change accordingly.

The first alternative—small alterations of the party system—represents a reproduction of the existing regime. The remaining two alternatives—based on changes in the pattern of political coalitions or cleavages and the social base of the state, with or without a change in the party system—represent a fundamental reordering of politics. Either would represent a critical juncture in Mexican politics.* How are we to assess the current changes in Mexico?

*In the comparative analysis of eight Latin American countries, Collier and Collier (1991) found that Colombia and Uruguay experienced a critical juncture

The first alternative should not be dismissed on the basis of the unexpected drama and excitement generated by the events of 1988. Indeed it is important to bear in mind the historical flexibility of the Mexican regime and its capacity to respond to challenge and regenerate itself through reform. We have noted above the history of electoral reform through which Mexican governments have given opposition parties greater representation without fundamentally changing the one-party-dominant regime, the underlying coalition of the party, or the support base of the state. Mexican political history also reveals regular projects to reform the PRI, though these have generally been aborted attempts. Even in past decades, then, the Mexican regime was not static, and its normal operation involved both flexibility and a dynamic pattern of reproduction or regeneration. In the 1980s and the 1990s, as we shall see, the role of opposition parties grew, the PRI undertook programs of party reform, and the government adopted constitutional amendments which changed the electoral system. In assessing these alterations, however, one must be aware that they do not necessarily mean fundamental political changes; rather, such modifications have traditionally accompanied the normal functioning of the stable Mexican regime.

We must also explore the possibility that Mexico may indeed be undergoing a critical juncture and a fundamental political reorientation. Though no one predicted the outcome of the 1988 elections much in advance, for some time now analysts have pointed to the soft spots of the Mexican regime and have cited various reasons for a crisis in PRI hegemony and a dissolution of the inclusionary governing coalition.

The most proximate of the causes for regime change is the debt crisis which began in 1982. Influenced in part by IMF conditionality, the policies pursued by the government of Miguel de la Madrid in response to the debt crisis made his term of office (1982–88) the first since the Revolution to record no economic growth. Austerity measures cut real government spending by over a third (*Latin American*

---

in which politics were reoriented but the party system remained essentially unchanged. In these two cases, the critical juncture of labor incorporation took place under the aegis of the same two-party system that had characterized nineteenth-century politics and continued to be the dominant feature of twentieth-century politics. In all the other cases, the party system changed, as labor was incorporated into new parties.

Weekly Report, 8 December 1988), the purchasing power of the minimum wage was nearly halved, the contribution of wages to national
income was significantly reduced, and unemployment soared. By
the time of the 1988 elections the government had established a
record of inflicting hardship rather than offering the usual material
benefits necessary for sustaining the inclusionary coalition. The result was an outpouring of discontent which was translated into votes
for Cuauhtémoc Cárdenas, who, in his rhetoric as well as his name,
renewed the radical populist agenda set aside by the government.

Longer-term causes have also been suggested, so that although
no one anticipated the stunning outcome of 1988, many analysts
had had a sense that a crisis in the Mexican regime had been
building for a long time. For about a decade before the 1982 debt
crisis, economic problems had been apparent, and one could find
evidence of a breakdown of the economic model under which
Mexico had enjoyed a long period of sustained growth. From the
early 1930s Mexico had achieved annual growth rates averaging
more than 6 percent, and the 1954 devaluation ushered in the period
of stabilizing development when this growth, based on a protectionist model of national industrialization and import substitution,
was maintained along with relatively stable prices. In the 1970s,
however, this pattern of success began to change. Growth was
maintained, but inflation rose to double digits, and capital flight
occurred as the government role in the economy expanded and in
other ways as well government policy destabilized the expectations
of the business community. By mid-decade Mexico had gone to the
IMF for help. The oil boom only postponed the crisis. With the end
of the pattern of stabilizing development, consensus around economic policy-making broke down, and the coalition represented by
the party could not be sustained so easily. Economic policy became
more zero-sum and hence inconsistent, as contradictory demands
were pressed by labor and capital. In the end the government had
a harder time pleasing either sector. The 1988 elections, as we shall
see, revealed major defections from the PRI by workers. A similar
development took place among an important part of the private
sector which had grown larger and more confident in the previous
decades. It withdrew from close cooperation with the PRI and went
on the political offensive both to take economic policy in a new
liberal or neo-orthodox direction and to seek political changes

which would dismantle the populist alliance (seen as the obstacle to rational economic policy-making) and liberalize the political system to allow its more direct political participation through an opposition party, the PAN.

Another longer-term cause of the 1988 electoral outcome and disaffection from the PRI was a change in social structure. Along with economic growth had come rapid urbanization, which meant both a decline in the peasantry, a pillar of support of the PRI, and a swelling of the urban informal sector, to which the party had not developed similar organizational links or attracted similar support. At the same time, the last decades saw an impressive growth in the middle class, which in the 1960s and 1970s may have as much as doubled its relative size to become more than a quarter of the population (Cornelius et al. 1989: 7). The middle class was at best imperfectly included in the one-party system, represented in the PRI through the organizations of its Popular Sector. Many in the middle class were becoming impatient with nondemocratic, authoritarian politics and the growing corruption in government which even by Mexican standards had reached scandalous levels during the oil boom in the government of López Portillo. The disaffection of this group could be seen in its growing support for the PAN.

Accompanying the social and economic pressures for a reordering of Mexican politics is a political one. Many analysts have pointed to the crisis in the regime's legitimacy stemming from the increasing implausibility of the official claims that the party embodied the popular revolutionary coalition. This symbolism was harder to maintain as the Revolution receded in history and as the meaning of the reconstituted coalition of the aftermath period, with its greater subordination of the popular sectors, became apparent in the skewed benefits of industrialization and economic growth. The legitimacy crisis was exposed dramatically by the 1968 massacre of hundreds of protesting students as Mexico prepared to host the Olympic games. The decade that followed saw the proliferation of many groups and organizations, particularly on the left, that rejected the political monopoly of the PRI and the influence it had in labor unions. The outcome of the 1988 election is often seen as an extension of these developments.

A final important factor is a change not internal to Mexico but in the international economy. At least since the 1970s the global capitalist economy has been reordered. The international economy has become more competitive at the same time that capital and production have been reorganized on a global scale with the rise of multinational corporations and a growth in world trade, so that countries have become more closely integrated into the international economy. A changing international division of labor has defined a relatively small group of countries that are the sites for foreign direct investment and a small group of newly industrialized countries (NICs) that occupy a niche of exporting manufactures, including quite sophisticated products based on high-technology production. Incentives therefore exist for some countries to acquire a high-technology capacity, attract foreign investment, and seek certain positions in the international division of labor by becoming efficient exporters—in short, to turn to an externally oriented economic model which has very different implications for domestic coalitions.

From all these perspectives, it has often been argued that the PRI and the hegemonic party regime had become obsolete. If it was at one time appropriate for a more rural, less industrialized, and poorer society in the context of an import-substituting industrialization model, changes in the social structure, a more advanced level of economic modernization, and the exigencies of a new economic model meant that the regime had outlived its usefulness and/or was failing to provide legitimacy and maintain the capacity to oversee a successful strategy for economic development and growth.

We shall consider politics in the 1980s with these questions of continuity and change in mind. As we have seen, the Mexican hegemonic party regime was sustained by a constant renegotiation of the coalition, differentially directing benefits and concessions as needed to maintain the system. Until the 1980s the regime generally had the resources to contain opposition and maintain the hegemonic party system. That is, up through the López Portillo government the regime seemed able to use the traditional means to contain dissidence and opposition that emerged at least in part as a product of the very dynamics of the regime itself. Even as late as 1988, the ability of the regime to control, manage, and coopt opposition movements was often considered so great that as the 1988 elections approached one interpretation suggested that the FDN, the opposition front put together by Cárdenas, was sponsored by the government to provide a bulwark against the rightist opposition of the PAN, which the government considered the more serious threat.*

As the 1980s opened, the Mexican regime did not seem poised for dramatic change. The same internal dynamics of the regime—the constant process of negotiation, conciliation, and cooptation on which it historically rested—were very much in evidence. Opposition movements continued to challenge the regime from outside, and pressures for reform emerged from inside; however, these were part of the dynamic of Mexican politics. By the end of the 1970s, some reforms had been initiated, particularly in the electoral system, but these seemed primarily to have reinforced the system. Reform projects continued to arise within the party, but not much came of these as vested interests prevailed and were able to defeat any challenge to its corporatist structure.

Even through the elections of 1982 the semi-competitive, party-dominant regime based on the inclusionary coalition seemed firmly in place. The electoral reform of 1977 reserved seats in the Chamber of Deputies for opposition parties at the same time that PRI representation remained overwhelming, as did its percentage of the national vote—about 70 percent in the elections of 1979 and 1982.

Furthermore, the position in the coalition of organized labor seemed secure as it continued to play its traditional role of supporting the regime in times of economic crisis and accepting hardship and belt-tightening in exchange for the expectations of future concessions and payoffs. In early 1982, the government devalued the peso, but the upcoming elections constituted one of those political moments of more effective demand-making by labor, so the government softened the full impact of the devaluation with a wage increase. In this way, the government was attentive to political exigencies and was willing to some degree to undermine its own economic policies in order to attend to the coalition with labor (Camp 1984: 548).

The 1982 elections took place in the midst of a mounting economic crisis that exploded shortly after the elections, when Mexico

---

*Similar interpretations have suggested that the foundings of the PPS, the PARM, and even the PAN were all supported by the government. I have also come across the interpretation that in the fraud perpetrated in the 1985 elections that was aimed at depriving the PAN of victories in the northern states, victories were assigned to the left opposition parties rather than to the PRI. Such interpretations may be less important for their accuracy than for their overall assessment of the PRI's capacity to manage events, manipulate situations, and perpetuate its hegemonic rule.

announced that it could not meet its obligations on international loans, which (like most Latin American countries) it had rapidly accumulated in the context of the flood of petrodollars in Western banks following OPEC oil-price rises in the 1970s. This announcement ushered in a full-fledged debt crisis throughout Latin America and more broadly throughout the Third World.

The new president, de la Madrid, signed an agreement with the IMF and adopted a tough austerity policy and a package of neo-orthodox economic measures that resulted in a dramatic decline in the real income of important sectors of the population, including labor. The opening moves during the new sexenio seemed to indicate once again that the old system was intact and that the Mexican hegemonic regime continued to afford the state the political resources for an impressive degree of autonomy in its decision-making and economic policy-making.

If at the beginning of the de la Madrid sexenio, the political regime seemed essentially intact, what happened over the course of the de la Madrid presidency that produced the startling and unexpected results of the 1988 elections? It would seem that the turning point in Mexican politics came in 1985, when a number of pressures for change that had been accumulating over several years came together in a way that caused a rupture in the existing pattern. The events in 1988 can be seen in light of this discontinuity, this process of change toward new coalition patterns, a different social base of the state, a new pattern of state-labor relations, and a more liberalized regime and more competitive party system which would institutionalize these changes. Two points must be emphasized, however. First, the identification of the mid-1980s as a turning point does not imply that either the debt crisis or the specific events of 1985 were sufficient or necessary causes. It would seem more accurate to conceive of them as triggers that accelerated a response to the social and economic changes that had been occurring for a long time and that had already produced a number of visible strains in policy-making and in the political regime and party system. Second, any potential retreat from the old political game and a change to a new one—to the extent it was or is being made—was perhaps not made definitively or irrevocably. The analysis will thus end with some remarks on this as yet open-ended situation in Mexico.

DE LA MADRID PHASE 1, 1982–85: SHORT-TERM ADJUSTMENT AND POLITICAL CONTINUITY

De la Madrid entered office at the end of 1982 in the midst of both an economic and political crisis. Economically the country was reeling under the impact of the debt crisis, begun four months earlier, when the government had declared its inability to continue to make interest payments to international lenders. Foreign debt was particularly large in the case of Mexico, which, with a long history of successful economic growth and vast newly discovered oil reserves, was especially attractive to lenders. In the early 1980s, sharply rising interest rates combined with falling oil prices to make Mexico the first among the debtor nations to enter financial crisis. Though the dramatic climax of the crisis occurred in August 1982, the signs pointing toward economic trouble had been sharply outlined from the beginning of the year, when the brief oil boom of 1978–81 came to a halt. Inflation was rising, and in February the government had found it necessary to devalue the peso. Shortly thereafter one of the country's major industrial groups, Alfa, staggering under heavy debt on which it now had to meet obligations with devalued pesos, was on the verge of bankruptcy. By the summer, in what was a rescue attempt of another private company, the government purchased shares of one of the largest construction groups and bought Mexicana Airlines (Camp 1984: 551–52). At the same time, inflation accelerated to a level that would officially amount to nearly 100 percent over the year, and capital flight took place at an unprecedented rate.

Politically the crisis was twofold. De la Madrid had been opposed by the labor sector of the PRI as too conservative and unsympathetic to the basic interests of labor. In the previous two presidential successions, the Labor Sector had been insulted by the failure of the outgoing president to consult it in the discussions leading to the choice of the party's next candidate, whose elevation to the presidency would be automatic in the hegemonic party regime. The choice of de la Madrid seemed particularly adverse to labor, and Fidel Velázquez took the unusual step of laying down conditions before he would accede to backing the party's candidate. The crisis with labor was mitigated by outgoing president López

Portillo's dramatic move to nationalize the banks in a desperate attempt to do two things: avoid the traditional shock medicine that was being prescribed by economists domestically as well as in the international community (including the IMF), and regain political support that seemed to be sapping not only his own waning presidency, but also potentially the office and the regime itself. The bank nationalization was wildly popular and immediately bought good will and mass support throughout the country—except of course from an important part of the private sector whose jitters and opposition to specific policies turned to outraged hostility. In this way, the crisis with respect to labor paled compared to that with the private sector as de la Madrid took office.

The joint political-economic crisis thus seemed to lead to the adoption of orthodox economic policies that would win the approval of international creditors and would at the same time begin the difficult task of rebuilding the confidence of the shaken private sector, whose cooperation would be central to any model of capitalist economic growth. In the first month of the de la Madrid presidency, the government concluded an agreement with the IMF and committed itself to the classic monetarist package that emphasized a sharp cut in the fiscal deficit, particularly through cuts in public spending, a contraction of the money supply, and an exchange rate adjusted to international market conditions. The result was the international acclaim of Mexico as a model debtor, along with a sharp recession that meant a 5.3 percent contraction in GDP and a fall in the purchasing power of the urban minimum wage and average industrial wages of about 25 percent in the first year alone (Roxborough 1989: 92; Kaufman 1988: 85, 93).

THE COALITION WITH LABOR

Though the adoption of economic orthodoxy and austerity, cooperation with the IMF, and a retreat from economic nationalism seemed like a departure, in many ways the opening moves in the de la Madrid sexenio represented business as usual—a continuation rather than a break in the familiar pattern of regime dynamics. As we have stressed, a striking feature of the Mexican regime was its capacity to impose economic hardship in the short run and even to achieve some understanding from labor on macroeconomic policy in times of crisis. With the enormity of the crisis during the de la Madrid term, economic hardship was indeed inflicted on labor. Not only did the purchasing power of wages plummet to a degree that was more severe than in Brazil and Argentina—the other two largest Latin American debtor nations—but also in 1981–84 the share of wages in national income dropped from 42.6 to 32.5 percent (Lustig and Ros, cited in Kaufman 1988: 92–93). At the same time, the recession threw many workers out of their jobs, and open unemployment surged upward. Nevertheless, the familiar understanding with labor was worked out. Particularly striking about the first years of the de la Madrid sexenio was the ability of the government once again to move decisively in the area of economic policy, to impose a level of hardship that only harsh, repressive military regimes had had the capacity to do elsewhere in Latin America, and to do it while maintaining social order.

This was not the first time the Mexican government had imposed short-run belt-tightening on labor. The implicit understanding in the Mexican system was that labor's cooperation during such times of crisis—whether it be the anti-fascist drive during World War II or the anti-inflation stabilization program in 1954 or 1976—would be accompanied by fairness, by some nonwage concessions (usually with respect to benefits, consumer subsidies, and political and organizational advantages), and by the future recuperation of losses.

It should be emphasized that the "understanding" with the labor movement did not take the form simply of the latter's readily acceding to government economic policy, for that does not describe the dynamics of the one-party-dominant regime in Mexico. Rather, the coalition and the understanding had to be reproduced, and this reproduction had two components. The first was government assurances to labor, and the second was conflict with the CTM. The assurances came in the stated commitment by de la Madrid to maintain social spending, increase levels of employment, and spread the hardship of the debt crisis equitably across all social groups. Furthermore, the government assumed that the economic "shock treatment" it was implementing consisted of a big dose of drastic measures that would rather quickly cure the patient and establish the conditions for renewed economic growth. The projections called for a difficult two-year period during which inflation and the debt-servicing burden would be brought under control and after which a recovery would begin. Renewed growth would begin moderately in late 1984, pick up to a rate of 3-4 percent in 1985, and sustain a rate of about 6 percent for the rest of the sexenio (Bailey 1985: 591).

The second component of the reproduction process was conflict between the government and the CTM, which opposed government policy. This conflict, which took place within well-defined parameters, was necessary to sustain the institutional viability of the CTM. In Mexican regime dynamics state-labor understanding was not readily or automatically achieved even with an "official" labor movement. Rather, it was the product of a political dynamic which was probably more than a mere charade, however predetermined the outcome seemed. CTM protest should probably be understood not simply as ceremonial or ritualistic or pro forma behavior on the part of corrupt, oligarchic labor leaders relatively unconcerned with the well-being of their constituency as long as their personal positions were secured, but also as a central dynamic of the process of negotiation, conciliation, and "pressure politics" occurring within a framework in which the existence or continuation of the state-labor alliance was not really in question.

The crisis began to unfold within the usual framework of state-labor relations. A series of steps can be traced out. First, in February 1982, when the crisis began to mount, the government (as noted) devalued the peso. The next month, government policy increased salaries between 10 and 30 percent, with lower salaries receiving a larger percentage increase. According to most observers, this concession on wages, which contradicted some of the intended benefits of the devaluation, was a response to pressure from organized labor (Camp 1984: 548) and reflected the inclusion of labor in the government coalition.

The second step occurred a year later, during the depth of the economic crisis as the de la Madrid government reoriented policy toward IMF-style orthodoxy and real wages began to plummet. The CTM, reflecting rank and file discontent, joined independent labor organizations in opposing government policy, not only with public statements, but also with industrial action and the threat of a general strike in May-June 1983 and again in the beginning of 1984. In a single week in June 1983, a CTM call for a 50 percent wage increase was backed up with 3,000 strikes (Roxborough 1989: 104). The CTM opposition was not a major departure from the past, but in fact fit the traditional pattern and was part of the basic dynamics of the Mexican regime. As we have seen, labor discipline was not achieved simply through coercion. Rather, even the official union movement had to engage in at least limited representation. In response to the pressure exerted by the CTM, the government attempted to weaken the confederation by favoring a rival confederation, the CROC. The government continued its hard line on wages through 1983 and 1984, with an adjustment in the minimum wage for the latter year that was lower than even that advocated by the private sector. Through all of this, the government benefited from CROC support of the austerity policy, its acceptance of wages lower than those demanded by the CTM, and its opposition to the CTM general strike calls. This CTM-government conflict and the use of the CROC as a rival support group was in many ways parallel to the pattern of conflict and negotiation that occurred in the context of the 1954 devaluation.

The final step in the reproduction of state-labor accommodation was worked out in 1984 and the first part of 1985. The CTM softened its oppositionist stance. Anticipating mid-year elections in 1985, the government for its part backed off somewhat from its austerity policy, resuming a somewhat higher level of public spending, stimulating the beginnings of a recovery, and offering some concessions. The renewal of the state-labor alliance took tangible form in April 1985, when the CT produced a document that indicated a shift from criticism and opposition to the formulation of an alternative policy, one which was very similar to that put forth by the CTM in 1978. Though the labor position called for wage indexation, it focused on nonwage measures that would protect purchasing power. According to Middlebrook, the document's "principal purpose was to reaffirm the historical importance of state-labour cooperation and state actions to promote socially equitable economic development." By the end of April, the government had reciprocated with concessions on the funding of union-owned consumer cooperatives and the provision of basic commodities, worker housing, training programs, credit, and an increase in worker profit-sharing from 8 to 10 percent (Middlebrook 1989: 205).

POLITICAL REFORMS

Other aspects of policy in the first phase of the de la Madrid sexenio also took place within the familiar terms of Mexican political tradition. By the end of the previous sexenio, confidence in López Portillo had plummeted, not only because of the economic crisis during his watch, but also because of unprecedented levels of corruption in which he personally participated. The lack of moral authority and a leadership crisis threatened the legitimacy of the regime itself. In response, de la Madrid centered much of his presidential campaign around the issue of the effectiveness and efficacy of political structures and emphasized moral renovation to attack corruption and electoral fraud, political reform, and decentralization. Early in his presidency, policies were indeed adopted that addressed these issues, but, particularly as the problems were not new—only perhaps more acute—the measures taken did not constitute a decisive break with past attempts.

The moral renovation campaign began early in the sexenio. New legislation addressed the problem of conflict of interest and signaled a tougher stance toward corruption on the part of public officials. A new federal agency and post of general controller were created to establish formal government oversight. Cases of corruption were prosecuted to underscore the seriousness of the issue. Though those targeted for prosecution were primarily middle-level officials, charges were also leveled against the heads of PEMEX (the state oil company) and the Federal District police (Camp 1984: 547; Bailey 1985: 586–87).

A particularly important concern that bridged the issues of moral renovation and political reform was that of electoral fraud, to which the PRI had previously resorted in order to prevent opposition victories, particularly for governors and senators, although most analysts would argue that it was unnecessary to maintain overall PRI dominance. At first, the government showed an unusual frankness and openness about the problem that constituted, among other things, an admission of past transgressions. State and local elections at the end of 1982 and during 1983 got the government off to a good start, with an unprecedented showing of opposition victories, particularly for the PAN in cities in the northern states. By 1984, however, some backsliding took place when the PRI engineered the ousting of a leftist opposition mayor in Juchitán, Oaxaca, and when the army was called in to respond to the violence that erupted surrounding charges and countercharges in connection with local elections in northern states (Bailey 1985: 589; Camp 1986: 545).

The government's announced commitment to clean elections was part of a larger program of political reform that would increase grass-roots involvement in electoral life and expand opposition representation at levels and arenas beyond the federal Chamber of Deputies (which had most recently been reformed in 1977). This larger reform program, which had roots as far back as 1963, has widely been interpreted as an attempt to strengthen the legitimacy and position of the PRI, not to introduce greater power-sharing or to supersede the dominant-party regime. One aspect of the program was municipal reform, which was begun under López Portillo and carried forward early in the de la Madrid sexenio. In 1983–84 a new municipal reform was put in place. It focused on two main areas: greater municipal autonomy, particularly in budgetary matters, and increased minority party representation in municipal councils. The municipal reform was not a departure, but rather a continuation of familiar themes of decentralization and expanded minority party representation in electoral bodies.

Electoral reform itself did not advance in the first half of the de la Madrid sexenio, although in 1984 two parties obtained legal registration: the PARM, which had earlier lost its registration because of its failure to maintain the requisite level of support, and the PMT. During these first years of the sexenio attention focused instead on reform within the PRI. Again, this was a continuation of earlier attempts to address the waning legitimacy of PRI-dominated government by bringing the party closer and making it more responsive to its base membership. This particular version was called "direct consultation with the mass base." Adopted by the party in the middle of 1984, it was an effort to introduce competitive party primaries as the basis for candidate selection at the local level, where they were deemed appropriate. As with the scheme of transparent democracy, which it resembled, it met limited success. In the following year and a half, local elections were held in 19 states, in which consultations were held in about 38 percent of the 1,211 municipalities (Bailey 1988: 116–18).

ECONOMIC POLICY

Economic policy, though clearly addressing the special circum-
stance of the moment, did not necessarily represent a major break
with the past. Certain features of economic policy-making stood out.
Responsibility for policy was clearly in the hands of "technocrats"
or *técnicos*—professionally educated holders of top cabinet and policy-making posts who rose through bureaucratic and administrative
ranks rather than political, party, or electoral careers. In response to
the debt crisis, the new technocratic team took politically difficult
and unpopular measures: the government reached an agreement
with the IMF and adopted the standard set of orthodox economic
measures. At the same time, it made a series of overtures to the
private sector following the dramatic bank nationalization on which
López Portillo left office. Technocrats had already begun to figure
prominently in the government of López Portillo, and the beginning
of his sexenio also saw attempts to reassure the private sector in the
wake of the Echeverría government, which had emphasized the use
of more populistic measures to attend to the political problems that
arose in the wake of the student massacres of 1968 and which had
ended in a similar crisis in state-private sector relations. A prior IMF
agreement and austerity package had also been initiated in the
mid-1970s before the oil boom had bought a way out.

In general, though the de la Madrid sexenio began in a burst
of energy with the adoption of a number of programs and reforms,
in many ways it could be characterized as a continuation of trends
that had been previously set in motion, and overall it did not break
new ground in terms of the basic framework of the dominant-party
regime of Mexico. The events of 1985 and their fallout, however, led
one to question if this pattern of continuity would persist or rather
if a new political game had been initiated.

DE LA MADRID PHASE 2, 1985–88: LONG-RUN RESTRUCTURING
AND COALITIONAL SHIFT

In the second half of 1985, four important events took place that
in retrospect may prove to be pivotal in Mexican political change.
The first was the mid-term elections of July. On the one hand, the

success of the PRI and the weakness of the opposition seemed to indicate that even under economic conditions that at the very least rivaled those of the Great Depression, the hegemonic party system remained in place and opposition parties were unable to capitalize on the hardship. While the PRI vote for the Chamber of Deputies was down from the over-80-percent level of the period before 1970, it showed only a moderate dip of less than 5 percentage points in 1985 compared to its level of support in elections after 1970 (from 69.3–69.7 to 65.0 percent).* Undermining the conclusion of continued PRI strength, however, was the crude form of electoral fraud perpetrated, particularly in (though not limited to) the states of Sonora and Nuevo León, where the PAN had a strong political base. The economic crisis, a leaked opinion poll the previous March, and the often overblown claims of the PAN, as well as the government's public commitment to clean elections, had led to the expectation of a better opposition showing and even some anticipation of an emerging two-party system based on the PRI and the PAN. In the context of these expectations and of close PAN-U.S. relations, the international press focused attention on the 1985 elections, giving unprecedented world publicity to—and perhaps even an overblown account of—the electoral fraud. The international delegitimation of the Mexican regime mirrored a similar internal process that centered on the party's unwillingness or inability to carry through a project of moral renovation and clean elections. This electoral fraud and its repetition in state and local elections in four states the following year led PAN leaders to adopt a new strategy of direct confrontation and violence (Bailey 1988: 169–71). Within the PRI, it led to a reposing of the issues of an expanded process of democratization.

After the 1985 elections, there was widespread assessment on the part of many observers of Mexican politics that the system had reached a point of no return. Rather than legitimating mechanisms, elections seemed to become delegitimating mechanisms. Though no one was able to foresee the course Mexican politics would take— even in the next presidential elections just three years hence—a typical assessment was that "Mexico's system of political parties and elections is . . . malfunctioning. It has lost much of its credibility and

*An exception occurred in 1976, a presidential election year in which, as noted, the PRI candidate was virtually unopposed and the PRI vote for the Chamber of Deputies returned to the higher level of 80 percent.

mass support" (Cornelius 1986: 141). Though most analysts predicted a gradual, incremental course of change in which the PRI
remained dominant and the PAN remained the major opposition
party, it was clear that the status quo would not persist.

The second pivotal event of 1985 was the devastating earthquakes that ravaged Mexico City in September. Besides putting an
obvious strain on the budget, these had the effect of further discrediting the Mexican government, and indeed the regime, in a number
of ways. For one thing, the disaster exposed a failure of leadership:
de la Madrid appeared weak, unable to take charge of the situation,
and even largely absent from public view at this time of tragedy. In
addition, the government response to the task of searching for sur-
vivors was criticized, particularly with international assistance agencies and the international press all focusing attention on and care-
fully scrutinizing the government role. The earthquakes further
exposed other aspects of government corruption in that government
buildings proved particularly vulnerable, casting doubts on building
code enforcement and construction contracts in the public sector.
Finally, in the void left by the government in the early stages of the
devastation, citizens of Mexico City organized themselves to meet
the disaster. Given the past capacity of the Mexican regime to fill
organizational space, this proved a rare instance of popular organization autonomous from government control or tutelage, and it had
the effect of empowering groups of citizens. It is interesting that
though the government eventually carried through an extensive
program to rebuild housing for the 150,000 who lost homes, this
largess did not apparently win many votes in 1988.

To the political shocks represented by the election and the
earthquakes can be added two economic shocks. First, after two and
a half years of tough austerity, the government had in mid-1984
eased up on the economic brakes, resumed a higher level of public
spending, and oversaw a slight recovery in the year leading up to
the July elections. However, in September—at the very moment of
the earthquakes—the IMF, in a dramatic disapproval of the economic
relaxation measures and the renewed inflation which accompanied
them, suspended the last payments under the old agreement because
of Mexican noncompliance. The other shock occurred in November,
when oil prices began to tumble downward. With these two events,
the optimism about economic recovery that opened the year soon

turned sour, and the recognition that Mexico had not pulled itself out of economic crisis—despite the severe austerity—could no longer be avoided. By the time the figures were tallied at the end of 1985, this relatively "good" year that had begun with a modest recovery presented the following picture: a growth rate of 2.7 percent that was virtually identical with the rate of population increase, an inflation rate of 63.7 percent (high by Mexican standards), an increase in government deficit to 9.9 percent of GDP, a drop in reserves, and a jump in capital flight (Cornelius 1987: 333).

These political and economic events in 1985 seem to have sparked a reorientation of Mexican politics. The first years of the de la Madrid sexenio seemed to be a continuation of the old pattern of maintaining the governing coalition by a kind of balancing act among sectors that revealed economic dependence on the private sector, with occasional swings that revealed political dependence on the popular sectors, particularly labor. The events of 1985, however, heightened the contradictions involved in that balancing act and led to the adoption of new positions both inside and outside government. There would be a move away from the old balancing act necessary to maintain a broad, inclusionary coalition toward a less "even-handed" approach that came down more heavily and decisively in favor of market-enhancing, neo-orthodox economic policy. As Robert Kaufman (1988) has suggested, what was notable about Mexican policy compared with that of Brazil and Argentina was the hard line it maintained with respect to economic orthodoxy, particularly at a time when those other two countries (Argentina in 1985 and Brazil in 1986) adopted new-style heterodox policies with the backing of the IMF and U.S. economic policy-makers. With this tipping of the balance toward economic orthodoxy and liberalization, the question became the impact on the maintenance of the integrative, hegemonic regime which the old balancing act had underwritten during the previous decades.

ECONOMIC LIBERALIZATION AND RESTRUCTURING

The failure of the economy to recover provided an important lesson: the orthodox shock treatment that Mexico had pursued since the beginning of the de la Madrid sexenio had failed as a short-run solution. The economic performance of 1985 disabused policy-makers and the public of the workability of a strategy based on a short period of orthodox stabilization measures and belt-tightening that would be quickly followed by renewed growth. A new approach would have to be found to reconcile the orthodox policies dictated by the debt with economic growth. The approach adopted was a commitment to longer-run, fundamental economic restructuring (Castañeda 1989a: B343). The ideas associated with structural reform were not new and to some extent had already been embraced by the economic team. Nevertheless, the post-1985 period saw a new commitment to this approach. Earlier policies had aimed at winning the confidence of the private sector, decontrolling prices, increasing private investment in ejidal lands, and encouraging foreign investment (Bailey 1985: 593). However, the earlier shift toward a free-market orientation intensified in 1985-86 (Cornelius 1987: 332). Economic restructuring would, on the most general level, redouble efforts to switch from an inward-looking, nationalist, protectionist, and state-interventionist model of import substitution to an outward-looking model of export promotion that sought to liberalize trade and integrate Mexico into the global economy, relying on the free market to make Mexican industry efficient and competitive. In 1985–86, Mexican economic policy saw not only the reimposition of harsh austerity measures that once again induced a deep recession in which the GDP fell by 4 percent in 1986, but also a more coherent, long-term commitment to economic restructuring and liberalization. In September 1986, de la Madrid announced that "Our austerity effort is permanent, but it now has a positive perspective of encouragement and growth" (cited in *New York Times*, 2 September 1986).

Consistent with the new emphasis was the decision about debt-servicing. As Mexico entered new, tough negotiations with international creditors after the collapse of the IMF agreement in mid-1985, the government seemed to raise the possibility of a new, unilateral approach to the debt, given the hardships the old pattern of restructuring had inflicted and the inability of the Mexican economy to support further payments. In the end, however, any departure was rejected in the renegotiation of an IMF agreement that was arduously worked out during 1986. Mexico agreed to continue in the long run the orthodox pattern that had proved an illusive solution in the short run: it agreed to restructure the debt and to continue to make interest payments with new lending, adding $13 billion of new debt (Castañeda 1989a: B341).

The emphasis on international opening also led to further measures toward trade liberalization. The first steps had already been taken toward dismantling the system of import licenses in favor of tariffs. By 1985 imports subject to licensing were reduced from 75 to 38 percent (Lustig and Ros, cited in Kaufman 1988: 88). After 1985, the elimination of barriers to trade was pushed much further. During 1987 tariffs were lowered to nearly 20 percent on most products (Castañeda 1989a: B343). In late 1985, reversing a decision of 1980, the government announced it would enter the General Agreement on Tariffs and Trade (GATT), concluding negotiations during the course of the following year. This decision was taken despite the opposition of labor and the weaker sector of private capital. It constituted a strong symbolic statement of a now formal commitment to economic liberalization.

The rededication to market mechanisms could also be seen in pricing policy, in which the government dramatically reduced subsidies and allowed prices to come closer to reflecting their free-market level. Though this process had begun earlier in conjunction with austerity policies and the need to reduce the state deficit, it now seemed to be part of a more coherent policy of economic restructuring and liberalization. In 1986 in particular there was a big jump in the price of public-sector goods and services and a reduction in government subsidies. With some important exceptions, the price adjustment occurred across the board and included basic consumer goods: utilities, urban transport, and even basic foodstuffs and staples such as tortillas, milk, and eggs (Castañeda 1989a: B345–46).

The extrication of the state from areas of economic activity and intervention could also be seen in the privatization of state firms. Again, the post-1985 policies took off from earlier programs, but this time with new meaning. In the first part of the sexenio, de la Madrid emphasized his commitment to a mixed economy and the central role of the state in directing or actively overseeing the economy. This was made explicit in the Immediate Project for Economic Reordering of December 1982 and reiterated in the National Development Plan of May 1983 (Bailey 1985: 590–91). With a pragmatic emphasis on state effectiveness, the 1983 program was a modest one. In 1985 the program was expanded, and in 1987–88 it was turned into "a vast, top-priority project" (Schneider 1988–89: 101). In 1985, 236 firms were put on the divestment list, but only 52 of these were operating enterprises; by mid-1988, mostly through sales and liquidation, the Mexican state had withdrawn from two-thirds of an expanded list of 765 firms. Mexico became a world leader in this retreat from state ownership—going much further than, for example, Brazil, which also claimed a commitment in this respect—and accounting for over a fifth of all privatized firms throughout the Third World and over half the divestment of all state firms, including forms other than privatization (Schneider 1988–89: 102). These figures may exaggerate the extent of economic liberalization and restructuring in Mexico since all the firms on the list accounted for only 3 percent of total production in the state sector, or 15 percent excluding PEMEX and the financial sector. In mining and manufacturing, however, they represented a reduction in state production of nearly one-third, and the state was retreating completely from the consumer durables sector (Schneider 1988–89: 102). The privatization policy must be seen not only as an element in a larger picture of economic restructuring, but also as a way to send signals to the private sector, improve the investment climate, and attempt to restore a good relationship with business groups. That is, privatization was in part a policy with political goals, a characteristic that could also be seen in its connection to state-labor relations, to which we shall return below. For the moment let us turn to the political fallout of the events in 1985.

POLITICAL REPERCUSSIONS

These events—the electoral fraud, the government's poor record after the earthquakes, and its failure to engineer an economic recovery—left the government so discredited that analysts widely referred to a legitimacy crisis not just of the de la Madrid government, but also of the PRI-dominated party regime. In this time of crushing economic hardship, it was the judgment of some that "Mexico's fundamental problem [was] not economic, but political" and that the Mexican regime was being transformed from a system of "electoral competition among adversaries into [one of] political struggle among enemies in which anti-system political parties act as the protagonists" (Alvarado 1987: 6–7). A change in the pattern of political conflict after 1985 could be discerned; it will first be examined in relation to changes on the part of opposition groups, then in relation to groups within the governing coalition—that is, within the government and within the PRI.

Effect on Opposition Politics. On the part of groups outside the governing coalition, the most important change was an increasing level of political opposition and conflict. On the right, the PAN was transformed from loyal opposition to a more militant, aggressive opposition party. This transformation had roots in the previous decade, but the real change came as a result of the events of 1985, in combination with the fact that the economic crisis had affected elements in the private sector in a way that favored the most militant faction (Maxfield 1989).

As we have seen, the result of the aftermath of radical populism had been to defuse private-sector opposition and restore a working business-state relationship within the overall context of a broad, centrist coalition that included the popular sectors. By the mid-1970s, the oldest and economically strongest industrial groups, strengthened by growth along the U.S. border of an in-bond, export-oriented "maquila" industry highly integrated into the global (particularly U.S.) economy, once again began to assert greater independence from and opposition to the government. Echeverría's renewed populism in the 1970s had set the scene for the new hostility of the private sector toward the government. While López Portillo, aided by the oil boom beginning in 1978, was able to smooth things over, the bank nationalization on which his sexenio ended opened a huge rift that would be an important feature of the de la Madrid administration. Open confrontation began to replace more discreet negotiation on the part of this more radical, northern faction. It took place on two levels: interest groups and political parties.

Three interest groups became important vehicles of private-sector opposition: CONCANACO, the peak commercial association; COPARMEX, the employers' association which, as we have seen, was founded at the end of the 1920s by the powerful Monterrey industrialists as a means to organize the private sector politically in the context of the impending federal labor law; and the CCE, founded in 1975, again at the initiative of the Monterrey group, to strengthen business-sector organizations in the face of Echeverría's populism. In addition to articulating their interests through such associations, these businessmen began to affiliate with and direct political action through the PAN, not only voting for its candidates, but also joining the party, backing it financially, and running on its ticket. The infusion of business interests in the PAN produced within it a *neo-panista* current that was the moving force of the transformation of the party. Initially the emergence of the neo-panistas caused a rift within the party, and in 1976 the impasse between the two factions prevented the party from settling upon a presidential candidate. In the 1980s, the neo-panistas increasingly set the tone.

With the bank nationalization of 1982, state-business relations had reached a new low. Given the dependence of the state on the economic cooperation of the private sector, the de la Madrid government undertook a number of policies to mend fences. It tried to protect the private sector from the full impact of the credit squeeze that came with the austerity program by creating new institutions that would expand the capital market (Camp 1984: 554); it adopted a number of liberalizing measures that had been on the agenda of the private sector; and it expanded communications and consultations with business leaders (Camp 1986: 555). In addition, it took steps to reverse and implicitly repudiate the bank nationalization to the extent politically feasible: in August 1983 it compensated the shareholders of the nationalized banks, and the following year it began to divest itself of the companies held by those banks (Bailey 1985: 592).

These moves, however, did not succeed in restoring good relations. Even as government policy moved closer to the economic liberalization advocated by much of the business community, private-sector relations with the government continued to deteriorate. Economically this was reflected in continued capital flight and low investment. Politically it was reflected in a changing attitude of part of the private sector. Increasingly business criticized not only government policy, but also the Mexican political system, because of what it regarded as the erratic policy swings that undermined investment planning and that could be attributed to the government alliance with labor. The most radical faction began to call for "political modernization" to limit the power of the presidency; to institute clean, competitive elections; to abolish the corporative system of interest representation within the PRI; and to increase private-sector input to decision-making (Cornelius 1987: 345).

In 1983 the criticism and opposition of the private sector escalated into a rupture in business-state relations. In the beginning of that year CONCANACO organized a conference in opposition to the bank nationalization and exchange control policy of López Portillo (Story 1987: 263), and the following year COPARMEX embarked on a more openly confrontational course when a new board of directors pointedly declined to invite the president to speak (as had been customary), accusing the government of being anti-democratic, statist, and pro-socialist. At the heart of its attack was the state-labor alliance and the social pact upon which all post-revolutionary regimes had been based. The conflict with labor that was contained in this position was manifest with the temporary ousting of COPARMEX from the INFONAVIT, the state agency for workers' housing, and labor's call for the cancellation of the legal registration of COPARMEX (Nuncio 1986: 118).

The rupture that began in 1983 could also be seen as businessmen moved more directly into the political arena to back PAN candidates in municipal elections. This contributed greatly to a new offensive of the right in that it at once politicized business groups in opposition to the government and led to a consolidation of power within PAN of the neo-panistas, transforming that party into a more militant, aggressive, confrontational electoral force on the liberal right.

From the beginning of the de la Madrid sexenio the PAN had been gaining in strength, particularly in the north. In 1982-83 it won important victories in municipal elections in five state capitals and in the ten largest cities in the state of Chihuahua—some by huge margins (Bailey 1988: 146; Cornelius 1987: 355). In the mid-term elections of 1985, according to official returns, the party's vote was nearly at an all-time high: only in 1982 had it done somewhat (two percentage points) better. However, the 1985 elections did not mark a great increase in PAN strength on the national level. The party captured only 15.5 percent of the vote, and this showing was not all that much better than the 11–15 percent it had typically won nationally throughout the 1960s and 1970s.

Nevertheless, if the 1985 elections did not represent an important turning point in terms of the relative electoral strength of political parties, these elections were significant in terms of the politics of electoral fraud. Though it is probable that fraud did not dramatically change the overall outcome—particularly on a national level—

it had a major impact in terms of the legitimacy of the political system, the tactics of the opposition, and the nature of political conflict.

Forewarnings of the 1985 fraud had been plainly visible. The PAN victories of 1982–83 had challenged the government's commitment to clean elections and its program of moral renovation. The first evidence of the weakening of the commitment to clean elections occurred as early as September 1983, when the PAN accused the PRI of using fraud in Baja California to prevent the first opposition victory for a governorship. In state and municipal elections of December 1984-January 1985, further charges of fraud erupted into violence in two cities in the northern state of Coahuila, as party militants were influenced by the more aggressive, confrontational stance of the neo-panista defense of the legitimate use of violence in such circumstances (Bailey 1988: 167, 170–71).

The reaction to the fraud during the September 1985 elections and the state and local elections that followed in 1986 was significant on several levels. Impetus was given to the formation of more concerted opposition movements. On the right (as noted), the private sector grew closer to the PAN, as did the Catholic Church (Cornelius 1987: 356). In addition, new forms of protest appeared. These included acts of civil disobedience such as hunger strikes and the blocking of bridges and highways. Another tactic was the use of the North American press to denounce the government. Following the 1986 elections, the Catholic Church announced the suspension of church services, a form of protest not used since the Cristero rebellion in the 1920s; however, the Pope intervened to call this off. On the left, the Communist Party had initiated a number of moves to achieve unity. In 1981 it had merged with minor parties on the left to form the Partido Socialista Unificado de México (PSUM). Subsequent attempts to broaden left unity failed. In March 1987, however, the PSUM and the PMT joined to form the Partido Mexicano Socialista (PMS). Though the PRT remained apart, the PRI was now faced with a reorganized left, capable of more concerted action.

Yet another result of the electoral fraud of 1985–86 was the crystallization of a rival legitimacy formula. Until that point, Mexico for all intents and purposes had only one legitimating political myth, and that related to the Mexican Revolution and the inclusionary coalition that was embodied in the PRI. Now, however, an alternative vision of democracy made inroads, emphasizing individual rights and the autonomy of civil society as opposed to the statist and corporatist vision of the PRI (Loaeza 1987: 103) Furthermore, though it was the PAN that presented this vision as part of its liberal critique and was able to do so most forcefully because of its greater electoral success, such a position could unite most parties on both the right and the left. It thus formed the basis of a PRI/anti-PRI cleavage which was given institutional form when the diverse opposition parties on all sides of the political spectrum united to form the Movimiento Democrático Electoral to denounce the 1986 elections and militate for clean elections in the future (Cornelius 1987: 356).

Electoral Reform. The events of 1985, the growing opposition to the PRI, and the challenge to the legitimacy of the one-party-dominant regime could not go unanswered. The government response was a new electoral reform.

Within the governing coalition there was a discernible split between those who, following a pattern established in 1963 to stabilize and recalibrate the political system, advocated a liberalization of the authoritarian regime, and those who insisted on maintaining the existing regime, using electoral fraud if necessary and distributing opposition seats as needed through negotiation rather than open electoral victory to preserve the PRI's overwhelming dominance. The former position was largely associated with the modernizing technocrats, who were gaining the upper hand with respect to economic policy and who indeed controlled the presidency. The modernizers saw political reform as a way both to include and thereby defuse the opposition and to enhance the popularity of the PRI by forcing it, in a more competitive situation, to come up with better, more representative, more popular, and less corrupt candidates. Particularly at a time when material rewards were unavailable because of the economic situation, a political opening seemed to be an important and effective move that would attract support and enhance legitimacy. The latter position was largely associated with políticos within the PRI—local and state political bosses and sectoral leaders (especially labor leaders) whose position was dependent on the perpetuation of the old system and who resolved any dilemma concerning collaboration with the government in favor of what had traditionally been a relatively privileged place in negotiations *within* the governing coalition.

At the beginning of the de la Madrid sexenio, those advocating political opening had the upper hand (Molinar 1989: 269). The result could be seen in the relatively clean elections of 1983 and recognition in those elections of opposition victories on an unprecedented scale. In reaction, local, regional, and sectoral leaders, who were most threatened by these victories, were largely responsible for the back-tracking that characterized the elections of 1984 (Cornelius 1986: 124–26, 134–35). The strength of the políticos was also evident in the conduct of the 1985 elections, though different explanations have been advanced. Some analysts attribute the 1985 fraud to the lack of conviction and loss of heart of the democratizers or liberalizers: given their inability in the economic crisis to rely to the usual degree on material distributions, they were unable to maintain popular support and resorted to fraud to achieve the electoral outcome they desired. Alternatively the fraud in the 1985 elections may have been largely the responsibility of the políticos, whom the liberal modernizers continued to oppose but were unable to control. No definitive study is available for choosing between these two explanations. However, the electoral reform which followed soon after the 1985 elections gives some weight to the second, though the evidence is inconclusive.

The 1985 electoral debacle, which was a blow to the legitimacy of the regime, dramatically posed the issue of political opening all over again. The 1986 electoral reform would seem to represent the reassertion of the liberal modernizers in the electoral policy arena at the same time that they were forming a more coherent, less compro-mising position in the economic policy arena. The electoral fraud in 1985 reversed the earlier move toward a political opening, and the result had been a blow to the legitimacy of the regime, despite the PRI's substantial electoral victory. The 1986 electoral reform repre-sented a step toward further political liberalization of the regime by increasing opposition representation. It did not, however, do so in a way that would prevent fraud in the future; indeed a major limita-tion of the new reform was the continued control of the PRI over the Federal Electoral Commission, which was responsible for over-seeing elections.

To interpret the 1986 reform, it is necessary to bear in mind the political situation as it appeared at the end of 1985. Two features are

worth emphasizing. First, because of the fraud of 1985 and the new①
form of militant reaction to it, the regime was in the throes of a
legitimacy crisis. The PAN had thrown up a substantial ideological
challenge, and the regime was widely seen as obsolete, unrepresentative, and undemocratic, despite election results showing that the
PRI was still the majority party by a wide margin—even accounting
for fraud. Some analysts went so far as to predict that the Mexican
system had reached a point of no return, though many others were
much more cautious about the implications. In any case, most as-
sessments were that systemic change, if it were to occur, would be
gradual and in the distant future (Needler 1987).

The second feature was that the electoral challenge to the ②
PRI—to the extent there was one—appeared to be not from the left
but from the right, and specifically from the PAN. The electoral
reform came when PAN opposition had reached new heights, with
its unprecedented electoral success of 1982–83, its closer affiliation
with private-sector groups, and the new militance and ideological
offensive of the neo-panistas. It furthermore came at a point when
the left opposition had been unable to capitalize on the economic
crisis and tumbling standard of living and when the CD was just
emerging as a reformist faction *within* the PRI and had not yet split
from the party (see below). Thus the electoral reform law was
promulgated at a time when the PRI seemed to be faced with only
the PAN as a potentially significant opposition force. Yet the threat
posed by the PAN was limited by its regional rather than national
base of support, and in any case it did not present much of a
programmatic challenge because at this very time the PRI government was moving to consolidate a liberal economic policy position
quite close to that of the PAN.

Most analysts have considered the 1986 reforms of minor significance. A closer look, however, may reveal some interesting shifts.
The logic of the previous reform of 1977 was to open the regime by
increasing the representation of small opposition parties, and at the
same time to inhibit the emergence of a second party that could be
a strong challenger to the PRI. The 1977 reform law made the
following provisions: 1) opposition parties were guaranteed a minimum representation of 25 percent in the Chamber of Deputies: 100
of the total 400 seats would be reserved for opposition parties
according to proportional representation (PR); 2) any party winning

60 or more of the 300 single-member constituency seats would be disqualified from the PR seats, or if opposition parties combined won over 90 single-member seats, only half (or fifty) of the PR seats would be distributed, thus barring not only the PRI, but also any medium or large party that might present more than a minimal challenge; and 3) each registered party in each of the plural PR districts would automatically be allocated one seat—a provision which further discriminated against the larger opposition parties and favored the smaller ones.

The logic of the 1986 reform seemed rather different. Whereas the 1977 law seemed especially oriented toward preventing the emergence of a strong second party,* the 1986 law seemed to reveal a greater acceptance of a stronger second party, though it guaranteed the existence of a majority party. The 1986 law had the following major provisions: 1) 100 PR seats were added, thereby increasing the overall representativeness of the Chamber; 2) it eliminated the ban from the PR seats of parties winning 60 or more majority seats, thus removing the discrimination against large opposition parties; 3) it increased the guaranteed minimum of opposition representation in the Chamber of Deputies from 25 to 30 percent by putting an absolute limit of 350 seats for any single party out of an expanded total of 500; and 4) a "governability clause" guaranteed majority representation of a single party by the straightforward provision of allocating the PR seats as needed to give the largest party a bare majority of 251 of the 500 seats. As long as the PRI won a plurality of the vote, it would have a majority of seats in congress.

It thus appears that the promulgators of the 1986 reform were willing to accept a more open, competitive system in which the PRI remained the largest party (and in which its majority status was guaranteed in times when it might fall to a plurality) and, within that constraint and distortion (as well as the distortion that comes from the single-member constituencies in both the Chamber and the Senate—since those types of electoral systems distort in favor of the largest party), an expanded and liberalized system of PR would be instituted to increase the representation both of the PAN and of the

---

*In the extreme case, a strong second party could win 59 majority seats and all 100 PR seats for a total of 159, but if it won one more majority seat, its total representation would be reduced to 60 because it would no longer qualify for the PR seats.

much smaller leftist and satellite parties. Because the 1985 elections revealed no defection of the popular sectors to the opposition, it seems likely that a party system was anticipated that consisted of a majority party, a second party which had a similar economic program and regional strength but which could approach only 20 percent of the national vote, and a host of much smaller parties, mostly to the left, but some of which would collaborate with the PRI. The result would be the continuation of essentially a PRI-dominated regime, but one with greater minority party representation and less discrimination against a challenging second party. Though the change may seem subtle, it could be interpreted as the beginning of a shift in the conception of the PRI from a dominant party in a one-party-dominant system to a majority party in a more competitive system.

Effect on the PRI. The political debate that intensified after 1985 and led to a consolidation of opposition to the PRI was mirrored within the PRI itself. Two contradictions became the source of intense debate in the years after 1985. The first, mentioned above, was within the economic model: how to deal with the problems of debt and inflation, on the one hand, and growth on the other. The second was between the economic model and the integrative, inclusionary political coalition.

The liberal neo-panistas vigorously and aggressively entered both of these debates, arguing that the economic problem was that government had not gone far enough in liberalizing the economy and reducing public spending and that it had failed to do so because it was too willing to accommodate its labor base and compromise its economic policy for political reasons. From this perspective, the complement to further and more consistent economic liberalization was political liberalization, which would benefit the PAN in elections free of fraud, sever the state-labor coalition, and enhance private-sector influence on policy. In many ways, this assessment had much in common with that of the de la Madrid government itself.

The economic debate was joined by groups critical of the government from the other side as well. According to the left opposition, the de la Madrid government had gone too far in adopting economic liberalization, opening the economy to foreign investment and freer trade, forfeiting economic growth, and abandoning those most economically vulnerable in favor of austerity, spending cuts, privatization, and the exigencies of debt-servicing. The orthodox shock treatment had failed in the short run, and the impact of such measures was too harmful to the popular sectors and too detrimental to issues of social justice to be sustained in the long run. Interestingly and probably more important, this critique by the left was also made by the PRI's traditional constituencies, which, after all, had been part of a large coalition based on economic nationalism and an interventionist state that to varying degrees had protected both national capital and the popular sectors. We shall return to the critique by labor below. For the moment, let us turn to the dissident movement within the PRI that came to be called the Corriente Democrática (CD).

The CD represented a reform-minded faction that was increasingly marginalized within the PRI. It opposed the hard-line economic policy of the government, the lack of political debate and input that surrounded its adoption, the inability of the government to maintain the legitimacy of the regime, and the failure of the party to carry through successfully the internal reforms which it had been attempting for the last two decades. The forces that would form the CD began to coalesce in the second half of 1985 under the leadership of Porfirio Muñoz Ledo, who in May 1986 led a group of workers, intellectuals, artists, and students in a march for national sovereignty. The following August the CD took shape and emerged as a force to be reckoned with. A number of PRI deputies, senators, and governors publicly declared their support for the CD and for what became its core project—the internal democratization and reform of the PRI. Cuauhtemoc Cárdenas, governor of the state of Michoacan, emerged as an important leader of the new movement and was able to bring peasant support not only from his home state, but also from areas where his father had carried out extensive land redistribution. The CNC, the national peasant association affiliated to the PRI, immediately declared its support; at the same time, Fidel Velázquez put the CTM on record in opposition, denouncing the CD as a threat to PRI unity—as he had all previous attempts of internal party reform.

During the next months, PRI leaders kept up a running dialogue with the CD, whose members were touring the country to gather support. In March 1987, however, the internal rift within the

PRI broke wide open. At a party assembly, the CD put forth its proposals for party reform and called for an "open process of consultation for the selection of precandidates" for the upcoming presidential elections. The head of the party, who had managed to unite the other factions of the party, embracing both the Echeverría and López Portillo factions, attacked the dissidents and asked them to "resign from our party and seek affiliation with other political organizations" (*Latin American Weekly Report*, 19 March 1987).

The split continued to widen, and in July members of the CD endorsed Cárdenas as a presidential candidate. Cárdenas accepted the nomination and began to tour the country. In August the PRI, in a symbolic gesture to the CD's demand for a more open nominating process for presidential candidates, announced six contenders, settling on Carlos Salinas de Gortari in the beginning of October. Shortly thereafter Cárdenas announced that he would oppose Salinas in the election as the nominee of the PARM. The PRI promptly expelled him from the party (*Latin American Weekly Report*, 29 October 1987). By the end of the year, the other parties that had traditionally been close to the PRI—the PPS and the PST—also moved to support Cárdenas, and a Cárdenas electoral front, the FDN, was formed. Thus at the same time that the government faced a new challenge from the private sector and the PAN on the right, it faced a new challenge from the left. By the end of 1987, a progressive faction within the PRI focusing on internal party reform was transformed into an opposition movement which had a wholesale critique of government policy and the dominant-party regime. The split dealt a serious blow to the integrative coalition which the PRI had held together: the new opposition was based on both a party faction within the PRI and the satellite parties which had previously lent the PRI support and legitimacy.

THE STATE-LABOR ALLIANCE

The more decisive move toward economic liberalization and restructuring after 1985 had important implications for labor and for the state-labor coalition. The new economic orientation clashed with the pattern of labor protection (however limited it may have seemed) that had characterized the post-revolutionary regime. Specifically, policies that promoted competitiveness and efficiency, the program of privatization, and the commitment to market mechanisms were at odds with the maintenance of real wage, employment, and unionization levels, as well as social welfare policies. Ultimately, both the technocratic policy-making style and the substantive policy orientation contradicted the state-labor alliance and the social pact which had been the bedrock of the Mexican regime. As Laurence Whitehead has suggested, the Mexican government

> adopted an increasingly "technocratic" rationality that conflict[ed] with the "patron-client" bargaining of past social pactmaking. . . . [T]he de la Madrid administration presided over a grave weakening of the [state-labor alliance, which] to some extent may have been an inescapable consequence of the post-1982 economic crisis, but . . . [which] also reflected a series of political choices . . . that were optional rather than inevitable (n.d.: 26, 37).

Indeed the change in economic orientation from a short-run austerity program to a long-run commitment to economic restructuring was accompanied by a change in labor policy. The government no longer sought to maneuver among labor organizations in order to secure support—or at least passive acceptance—of short-run belt-tightening; rather it began to contemplate a long-run alteration of the state-labor coalition in a fundamental political restructuring.

After 1985, then, the strain in state-labor relations intensified, as labor came to be seen less as a political ally and more as an obstruction to the goal of structural economic reform. A clash in policy orientation could be observed on a number of fronts. Labor demands ran counter to the government's attempt to fight inflation, which in 1986 and 1987 reached new and alarming heights;* to its attempt to reduce spending—after 1985, the government was less willing to exempt social programs from budgetary cuts; and to its commitment to reduce subsidies, stimulated not only by an effort to reduce the deficit, but also by a new commitment to the free market. As we have seen, the Mexican regime had been underwritten by an

---

* In these years, official figures registered the first triple-digit inflation. The 106 percent of 1986 represented a failure of previous stabilization attempts, though not a dramatic increase over the previous high in 1982. However, the rise to 144 percent in 1987 seemed to reveal a process out of control.

economic policy compatible with protecting employment levels, particularly in state enterprises, and with real wages that at different stages either held their own or rose in line with productivity increases, at least until the economic model ran into trouble toward the end of the 1970s. In the 1980s that policy changed. In line with an import-substitution model, the working class had been seen in terms of both a factor cost of production and a market for the product; with the turn to an outward-oriented economic model that focused on efficiency, labor increasingly came to be seen as only the former.*

The customary recuperation of real wages did not occur after the wage squeeze of 1982–85. Instead, real wages continued to tumble. Following the dramatic plunge from 1982 to 1985, government policy oversaw a further erosion of real wages during the rest of the de la Madrid sexenio. Having fallen about 23 percent from 1982 to 1985, the purchasing power of the urban minimum wage repeated that decline in the remaining years of the sexenio (*Comercio Exterior*, February 1990). Average wages in manufacturing, which had plummeted an even more dramatic 38 percent in the initial period, continued to slide downward in the second half of the sexenio (United Nations 1989: 60).

In addition, the government's policy of privatization was at odds with labor interests. Privatization was seen as impeded by the terms of labor contracts that resulted from the "very special relationships" most state enterprises had developed with their workers. These contracts, which were favorable to workers primarily in terms of fringe benefit packages rather than wages (which in real terms had been declining over a number of years), made the state companies unattractive to potential buyers in the private sector (Castañeda 1989a: B344).

At the same time that the government saw its traditional relationship with labor as an obstacle to privatization, the move to dismantle the state sector in turn was a way to alter that relationship,

*Data from Esthela Gutiérrez Garza (1988: 146–54) show that after a period in which nominal wages followed the rate of inflation and from the end of what we have labeled the conservative reaction of the aftermath of incorporation (that is, from the 1950s), real wages (both the minimum wage and wages in manufacturing) rose steadily. Gutiérrez Garza argues that this pattern was the result of government policy, which sought to maintain a high level of domestic consumer demand. This policy was supplanted in the 1980s.

get around labor contracts, and retreat from its former employment policies, in view of its rearranged priorities. A case in point is the closing of a state-owned steel foundry in Monterrey in May 1986 and the consequent elimination of 10,000–15,000 jobs. With this act, the government abandoned the priority it had given to the creation and maintenance of jobs—precisely the commitment upon which it had acted a decade earlier, when it had originally taken over the foundry (Cornelius 1987: B348).

As noted above, the period following 1985 saw an open debate about the direction of economic policy. On one side of the debate, the right, which had emerged from 1985 as the strongest source of opposition to the government, was strident in its anti-labor attack. In addition to advocating economic policies detrimental to labor, it took particular aim at unions, and COPARMEX called for the destruction of the CTM and the CROC (Trejo Delarbre 1987). As key liberal modernizers within the government drew nearer to the position of the right and the vocal private sector in this debate, they also began to give voice to a hitherto unutterable view that constituted an attack on the state-labor coalition—and ultimately the inclusionary regime based on negotiation and conciliation. Some within the government expressed the view that labor leaders not only misallocated resources and impeded economic restructuring, but also abused the privileges and concessions they received. The labor movement was seen as a source of corruption, gangsterism, and featherbedding, at the same time that it failed to get benefits for its members or mobilize their support (Whitehead n.d.: 29–30). The new anti-union sentiment led some to advocate a change in the labor law to weaken unions—for instance, by the elimination of the union shop (Middlebrook 1988: 139).

Indicative of the new attitude was the way the government handled some of the important strikes of the period. In February 1986, in violation of Article 123 of the Constitution, the government declared illegal a strike for higher wages by autoworkers at the Dina and Renault plants and sent the strike leaders to jail for seven days (*Proceso*, 10 March 1986). In February–March 1987, the government broke strikes among electrical and telephone workers (see below). While it had become nearly routine for the government to move against industrial action by workers in dissident unions, this episode represented a move against important "official" unions participating in a strike that had wide support and that had as its aim an increase in wages comparable to that already granted to the minimum wage (*Proceso*, 9 March 1987; Whitehead n.d: 31). The following July a strike at Ford ended with the dismissal of 3,200 workers as the company developed plans to automate (*Latin American Weekly Report*, 8 October 1987; Middlebrook 1988). Thus in 1986–87 relations between the government and labor deteriorated, as the government committed itself to economic restructuring that emphasized low wages, efficiency, firm flexibility, market discipline of the work force, no or weak unions in the booming maquila (in-bond) sector, and a streamlining of employment in traditional sectors (Trejo Delarbre 1987: 37–64).

On the other side of the economic policy debate were the traditional constituencies of the PRI. As noted, opposition to the policy of economic restructuring and liberalization was expressed within the PRI not only by the CD, but also by sectoral interests, particularly labor. As Jorge Castañeda has emphasized, the traditional constituencies continued to support the more nationalistic, protectionist, state-sponsored economic orientation:

> It was not primarily the Left outside the PRI that gave substantive support to all of these things nor opposed closer economic and perhaps even political ties with the United States. A significant part of the political establishment itself backed nationalistic policies and opposed opening up and ensuing closer alignment with the United States. What Muñoz Ledo, Cárdenas, and their small group of followers essentially were saying—on behalf of, although without the support, agreement, or representation of large sectors of the bureaucracy, labor unions, and the Mexican intelligentsia—was that they opposed those policies (1989a: B349)

Labor opposition to government policy prior to 1985 has already been noted above. In 1983, Fidel Velázquez had been an outspoken critic denouncing the policy as one which "primarily favored industry while the working class . . . remained in extreme poverty." As the 1985 elections neared, however, the veteran labor leader turned his attention to what he perceived as the greater threat posed by the PAN and the "electoral advances of the reaction" (*Proceso*, 25 May 1987). After these elections and with the new government commitment to economic restructuring, Velázquez once again took to the opposition and became increasingly harsh in his criticism. In the beginning of 1986 he persistently called for an emergency wage increase, and a rift with the government again opened. According to the newsweekly *Proceso*, Velázquez became "radicalized" in his pronouncements, and in November 1986 he declared the government's program "unacceptable" as it "puts into danger the viability of our national project" (*Proceso*, 25 May 1987).

These last words hold the key to an interpretation of Velázquez's position—i.e., opposition to the new economic orientation and a defense of the status quo ante, in both its political and economic aspects. His stance represented a repetition of the familiar pattern of labor tactics seen most recently in 1983–85: the CTM and the fidelistas could tactically threaten a rupture but in the end could not really risk one. Instead this dominant faction of labor continued to opt for a state-labor coalition as the best source of leverage. After 1985 this position seemed actually to be reinforced by the change in government orientation and the "new social equilibrium" toward which the regime was moving (Trejo Delarbre 1980). Rather than see in the new situation a cause for change toward greater independence from the government, the fidelistas instead seemed intent on fighting a rear-guard action to preserve the state-labor coalition in the face of an assault from the right—not only from the PAN, which in 1986–87 still appeared as the major opposition to the PRI, but also from the technocrats within the PRI and the government. In other words, the fidelistas were presented with not only an unfavorable economic policy, but also the possibility of a new political project to exclude labor from the governing coalition and abandon it to the discipline of market forces. In this situation, the move to open confrontation over economic policy was particularly tricky from the point of view of the fidelistas, who saw advantages to the historic pattern of bargaining within an inclusionary coalition.

The fidelista position was not the only one within the labor movement. Indeed a division opened up within the CT over the question of labor orientation toward the government. In the beginning of 1986 Francisco Hernández Juárez was rejected as president of the CT in favor of someone who represented a position more independent of the government. Within a year, however, the fidelistas were able to reassert their dominance within the union movement, and in January 1987 Hernández Juárez became president (Trejo Delarbre 1987).

Throughout 1987, the labor movement under fidelista leadership played a complicated game. It continued to press its economic and wage demands and to oppose government economic policy at the same time that it tried to maneuver politically to maintain—or restore—its bargaining position within an inclusionary government coalition. This last took two forms. First, it meant opposition to the Corriente Democrática, for the old game based on negotiation and conciliation was consistent with the application of pressure through strike action but not with political opposition and association with a minority party; it was a game internal to the governing coalition. Hence although the CD in many ways articulated the program of labor, labor leaders did not see fit to identify with it, particularly since its viability remained unknown. If the first part of the strategy implied the maintenance of a coalition with the dominant part of the PRI, the second part was an attempt to influence the central tendency of the PRI. Specifically, labor was anxious to influence the choice of the party's presidential candidate for the 1988 elections, and particularly to prevent the naming of Carlos Salinas de Gortari, the minister of budget and planning and a key author of much of the government's restructuring program. Both the fidelistas and Joaquín Hernández Galicia, head of the oilworkers union, vigorously opposed Salinas for his involvement in attempts to streamline the petroleum sector, break up the PEMEX monopoly, and weaken the oilworkers union (Grayson 1988). Instead of Salinas, labor preferred Alfredo del Mazo, minister of energy, mines, and parastatal industries.

The political strategy adopted by labor was not successful. In the face of the government's commitment to the new economic line, labor failed to demonstrate its indispensability as an ally. In March 1987, the electrical workers' strike was ruled "nonexistent" by the Federal Conciliation and Arbitration Board, and the government intervened to prevent the suspension of electrical service, despite the fact that most of the labor movement and the political parties, except the PAN and PARM, supported the strike. In reaction, the CT made demands similar to those of the electrical workers and threatened strikes against twenty parastatal companies. Some within the PRI suggested that this move had a political as well as economic motivation, and that was to boost the credentials of del Mazo by giving him an important and highly visible role in negotiating a settlement in the parastatal sector. If so, this too backfired, as Salinas was appointed to the official negotiating commission (*Latin American Weekly Report*, 12 March 87 and 9 April 1987). In October, Salinas received the PRI nomination for president.

In the face of this failure, the labor movement found itself in a difficult position, unable to devise an effective political strategy. Nevertheless, some accommodation was reached between the government and a weakened labor movement. In November and December, the Mexican economy took a sharp turn for the worse, with a stock exchange crash following that of the world's major markets, a halting of the debt-equity swap program, a disappointing outcome of negotiations with the United States over trade and investment, renewed capital flight, a devaluation of the peso, and a resurgence of inflation (*Latin American Weekly Report*, 12 and 19 November, 3 and 10 December 1987). The CT threatened to call a general strike. In the politically sensitive time of the approaching election, in which the PRI presidential candidate was the author of an economic program which in many ways seemed to be coming apart, the government entered into negotiations with labor and business representatives.

The December negotiations produced a tripartite agreement, the Economic Solidarity Pact, in which the signatories agreed to an economic package. The pact can be seen as a PRI strategy by which it seemed to address the social tensions unleashed by the policies of austerity and restructuring in order to reconsolidate the traditional coalition. That labor leaders signed was further indication of the way in which most of them tenaciously clung to the old strategy of attempting to bargain and negotiate from within the governing coalition. At this point, the Cárdenas campaign remained difficult to assess. Not only the labor leaders, but also the traditional left—the PMS and PRT—refused to back him. In this context, but with considerable dissension, the labor leaders signed the pact, despite misgivings. The left parties, the Cardenists, and independent trade unions immediately formed a front to oppose it (*Latin America Regional Report: Mexico*, 18 February 1988). Even labor leaders who had participated in the pact wasted no time in expressing their dissatisfaction.

All in all, the pact revealed the strength of the government and private-sector interests represented by the CCE, as well as the relative weakness of business interests representing smaller firms, which were opposed to both the opening to foreign competition and the provision for wage indexation. It also revealed the political marginalization of labor, which had to retreat significantly from its demands and received very little protection from the pact (Whitehead n.d.: 26; *Latin American Weekly Report*, 7 January and 3 March 1988). There seemed little doubt that during the de la Madrid sexenio, the political position of labor had deteriorated substantially and the state-labor coalition and the social pact upon which it was based had been severely undermined.

1988 ELECTIONS

By the beginning of 1988, there was cause for tension within the PRI coalition. The economic picture remained bleak, and most sectors of the population—particularly the traditional constituency of the PRI—had suffered enormously. De la Madrid had cut the fiscal deficit by 10 percent of GNP—something no other country since World War II had been able to do and certainly far more than what the United States was concurrently attempting with the Gramm-Rudman Act. At the same time, Mexicans' standard of living plunged, as by 1987 consumer prices rose to 13.8 times their 1981 levels and national production registered a slight decline while the population rose 15 percent (Luis Rubio, *Los Angeles Times*, 24 June 1988; Robert Samuelson, *Los Angeles Times*, 15 June 1988). Yet though labor seemed politically restless, it had gone along with the Economic Solidarity Pact. Thus the PRI had some house-cleaning to do to put its coalition back in order, but no one doubted its ability to do so, and numerous opinion polls seemed to confirm the party's expected electoral success later in the year.

The national election results in July 1988 thus had not been predicted at the beginning of the year, though the momentum of the opposition built up during the intervening six months made anything seem possible. The PAN, the principal source of opposition throughout the decade, seemed to be picking up support along with its greater militance. The new force on the scene, of course, was the candidacy of Cuauhtémoc Cárdenas, who with his two names was the personification of the most important popular symbols in Mexican political life: the nation itself, with its pre-Columbian roots, and the Revolution, the promise of which was fulfilled only in his father's government in the 1930s. Cárdenas's message of nationalism and populism—emphasizing such themes as social justice, the unacceptability of the debt burden, and the need for renewed growth in which all could participate—was an antidote to and rejection of the policies of the de la Madrid government. By any account, his success in the elections was impressive. The coalition that supported him easily surpassed the appeal of the PAN and became the second political force in Mexico, one that at the very least could rival the PRI itself.

Three points about the 1988 elections are worth emphasizing. The first is the stunning rise of the opposition, combined with the relative unity it achieved in confronting the PRI. The Cárdenas candidacy quickly unified around it the three satellite parties hitherto more likely to offer the PRI cooperation than opposition (except in some local elections). These were the PARM, the original vehicle through which Cárdenas declared his candidacy; the PPS; and the PST, which saw fit to change its name to the Partido del Frente Cardenista de Reconstrucción Nacional (PFCRN). The left-of-center alliance formed by these parties to advance the Cárdenas presidential bid, the FDN, initially failed to attract the traditional left, which had shown interest in a united effort and had itself taken important steps in that direction with the formation in 1987 of the PMS. Furthermore, Heberto Castillo, the PMS presidential candidate, had earlier appeared to invite Cárdenas to leave the PRI and run on the PMS ticket. However, Cárdenas's decision to opt for the PARM was unacceptable to the PMS leadership, who then refused to jump on the bandwagon. Even more recalcitrant was the PRT, which had also refused to join the PMS and which regarded the Cárdenas movement as "dissident priísmo" (*Latin American Weekly Report*, 16 June 1988).

This resistance by PMS and PRT leaders was challenged by an anti-government mass movement that unfolded as the FDN campaign quickly picked up momentum. Huge demonstrations in support of Cárdenas took place in February in Laguna, where his father's agrarian reform had had a big impact, and in March in Mexico City, where over 200,000 enthusiastic supporters turned out. The magnitude of popular outpouring against the government's economic policies and the authoritarian nature of the regime became clear during the rest of the campaign, as the Cárdenas candidacy became the focal point for a "social rebellion" on the part of students, youths, intellectuals, workers, and peasants (Anguiano 1988: 26, 33). This momentum precipitated a rift within the traditional left, as many groups within it changed allegiance to make common cause with the FDN. By March, the Movimiento al Socialismo (MAS) was launched by dissidents in the PMS, PRT, and other leftist groups in order to support Cárdenas. In the end, the PRT stood firm, but with just about one month left of the campaign, Castillo withdrew his candidacy and the PMS endorsed Cárdenas.

In addition to achieving virtual unity on the left, the opposition made common cause against the PRI through concerted action in which the PAN, FDN, and PRT tried to ensure clean elections. The Asamblea Democrática para el Sufragio Efectivo formed by the opposition parties was indicative of the importance of this issue and of the system/anti-system cleavage (Gómez and Klesner 1988: 4). This point should not be overstated: the cooperation among opposition forces was uneasy, and they hurled some accusations of electoral fraud at each other as well as more extensive ones at the PRI. Nevertheless, the PRI faced an unprecedented alignment of opposition groups monitoring the elections. While in the end joint vigilance and coordinated action did not prevent electoral fraud, the opposition's concerted action seemed to undermine the PRI's ability following the election to fall back on its old method of allocating at least some seats by negotiation with particular parties rather than by actual vote tally.

The second point about the 1988 elections was the stunning loss of legitimacy of the PRI-dominated regime. According to official returns, the party, by less than a percentage point, barely eked out a majority of the vote for Salinas—compared to virtually three-quarters of the vote obtained by de la Madrid six years earlier. In the context of the Mexican regime, these returns amounted to more than the loss of popularity for a particular party. Given the identity between the PRI and the regime—that is, given the status of the PRI as the "official" party in a one-party-dominant regime—opposition to the party and a loss of its popularity reflected a more general loss of overall legitimacy for such a regime.

Beyond the weak showing of the PRI, the 1988 elections repudiated the regime in a number of other ways. The first of these was the reaction to what was at the very least the appearance—if not the certainty—of massive electoral fraud. The interruption of the computerized returns (supposedly because of electronic failure), discarded ballots discovered in rivers or found burned, and a whole litany of techniques of machine politics which have added a colorful vocabulary to the Mexican political lexicon have been widely discussed in accounts of these elections. How massive the fraud may have been in actuality is open to question. Some analysts claim that given the unprecedented lack of popularity of the PRI, in combination with its well-honed techniques of what is known as electoral "alchemy," these elections were the most fraudulent ever. Others claim that given the close monitoring of the opposition in many areas and the number and nature of the charges of irregularities, these were among the cleanest of Mexican elections, and in any case the extent of the fraud probably did not change the overall results—at least not very much.

What seems irrefutable is the precipitous drop in PRI support from overwhelming to less than the officially reported majority of only a fraction of a point over 50 percent. Furthermore, while it is *possible* that the party, even if it could no longer attract a majority of the vote, had managed to retain a plurality, it could never legitimately make the claim that it had done even that. With documented cases of fraudulent practices and the refusal of the government to make public the returns of nearly half of the individual polling places (only district-level tallies were released), the PRI could not defend itself against the FDN contention that the government had stolen the election for the PRI and that Cárdenas in fact had won the plurality. As long as the FDN contention remained unanswerable, a legitimacy crisis existed centering around the question of the representativeness (or lack of it) of the regime. In other words, the legitimacy crisis attached not only to the outcome of this particular election, but also to the regime itself—to the PRI's role as the official party and to the whole gamut of arrangements (from access to the media to the composition of agencies that oversee the electoral machinery to the electoral system in both chambers of the legislature) that affected the democratic representation of parties.

The third point about the 1988 electoral results concerns who the winners were. The PRI, of course, officially emerged with a majority—but only barely. Its percentage vote for the majority seats in the Chamber of Deputies was nearly identical to that for president at 51 percent. This vote produced a huge majority of PRI deputies in single-member districts—234 of a total of 300 (78 percent). Another 26 seats were allocated to the PRI through the rules of proportional representation, for a total of 260—or a meager majority of 52 percent of the entire Chamber—essentially equal to its officially reported national vote tally (*Proceso*, 5 September 1988).* In the Senate, the PRI won overwhelmingly but ceded—for the first time—4 seats to the opposition. Despite this outcome, there are many ways (as mentioned above) in which the PRI could be seen only as the big loser rather than the winner.

The PAN was also a loser. Whereas before 1988 it had presented the only potential challenge to the PRI, it emerged from these elections far behind the FDN. What had earlier appeared as the PAN's growing strength now seemed more regionally limited. Only in the single-member constituencies in the Chamber, where it could take advantage of the geographic concentration of its support, did the PAN come out ahead of the FDN. Thus it won 38 (12.7 percent) of the 300 majority seats in the Chamber, outstripping the 28 seats (9.3 percent) won by the FDN parties (*Proceso*, 5 September 1988). In general, however, the PAN proved unable to capitalize on the hemorrhaging of PRI support in these elections. According to official returns, its 17 percent of the presidential vote was up only very slightly over 1982 (16 percent), although it represented a continued increase over the 11 and 14 percent it had won in 1964 and 1970 respectively. (It ran no presidential candidate in 1976.) In the Chamber, the national results with respect to *votes* (as opposed to seats) for majority districts were parallel, with similar levels of support and a similar inability by the PAN to significantly surpass its previous peaks: in 1988 it won 18 percent of the votes, compared to 17.5 percent in 1982 and 15.6 percent in 1985 (*Latin American Weekly Report* and *Proceso*, 18 July 1988). In the distribution of

*These results reflect those announced by the Federal Election Commission. Subsequently minor changes occurred when one elected *priísta* holding a majority seat defected to the FDN and the Electoral College, which has the power to make the final decisions concerning the official results, restored the PRI total by awarding it an additional proportional representation seat, thereby depriving the PPS of one. Some time after these last results were announced, 3 FDN deputies defected to the PRI. As a consequence of these changes, the PRI had 263 seats, the FDN was left with 136, and the PAN remained at 101, with the overall percentage distribution of seats hardly changing at all.

proportional representation seats it was allocated 63, as against 110 for the FDN parties.

The big winner was the FDN. Claiming a plurality of 42 percent of the vote, it was officially awarded 31 percent in the presidential race and 29.2 percent in majority districts for the Chamber of Deputies (*Proceso*, 12 and 18 July 1988). Because of the way in which an electoral system based on majority districts discriminates in favor of large parties (the PRI) and parties with geographically concentrated support (the PAN), FDN parties won only 9.3 percent of these seats, though they won the four Senate seats given up by the PRI. Once the proportional representation seats were allocated, the FDN parties held 27 percent of the total seats in the Chamber.

It is interesting to examine the relative success of the constituent parties of the FDN. The big victory was scored not by the traditional left—i.e., the PMS—which essentially maintained its past level of support, but by the satellite parties. That is, just as the Corriente Democrática was a dissident movement that split from the PRI and was able to unify those parties which, in different ways, also represented dissident priísta movements outside the party, so the voters attracted by the FDN cast their ballots for those parties rather than for the PMS, which belatedly also participated in the FDN. Within this pattern of the greatest increases in support being registered by the satellite parties, the most successful were those to the left rather than to the right.

Thus, whereas the PPS, the PST/PFCRN, and the PARM had won (in descending order) 1–1.5 percent of the presidential vote in 1982, these percentages increased to 10.5 percent for each of the first two and 6.3 percent for the last in 1988. By contrast, PSUM/PMS failed to improve its showing, winning 3.6 percent of the vote in 1988, essentially repeating its 1982 showing of 3.8 percent (*Latin American Weekly Report*, 28 July 1988). In the elections for federal deputies, where the vote could not directly attach to Cárdenas personally, the satellite parties did only slightly less well and the PMS slightly better, and the pattern observed in the presidential returns was repeated. The three satellite parties, having won less than 2 percent each in 1982 and 1985,* increased their relative support to 9.4 percent for the PFCRN, 9.2 percent for the PPS, and 6.1 percent

*In 1985 the PST won 2.5 percent.

for the PARM, while the PMS won 4.5 percent—similar to earlier showings of 4.4 percent (1982) and 4.8 percent (1985) (*Proceso*, 18 July 1988). The distribution of seats in the Chamber was not too different: the three satellite parties each won 6.2–6.8 percent of the seats, with an additional 4.6 percent held by coalition candidates, primarily PPS-PFCRN. The PMS did somewhat less well, with 3.8 percent of the total seats, reproducing its usual showing.

Chapter 5

AMBIGUITIES AND CONTRADICTIONS

How are the changes inaugurated under de la Madrid to be understood? Have social and economic changes accumulated to the point that they may be triggering a major political reorientation, and were the 1988 elections a dramatic expression of a new critical juncture in Mexican politics? Are we witnessing in the present period a fundamental change in the inclusionary one-party-dominant regime which included labor as a central base of mass support?

Analysts have emphasized the forces of both continuity and change. On the side of continuity, it is clear that the social pact with labor has been endangered, but many have found it hard to see how the PRI could afford to relinquish this traditional constituency. It has also often been pointed out that the PRI has suffered previous schisms, yet the government had resources to overcome them. Indeed in the first two years or so of the new sexenio, Cardenist forces had their share of trouble, and the long-term effectiveness or role of the new party they founded was far from clear.

On the side of change, a number of factors have been emphasized: the underlying demographic changes of growing urban middle and "marginal" classes, among whom PRI support has been relatively weak; the assessment of some that the economic policies of de la Madrid and subsequently Salinas did not stop at endangering the social pact with the popular sectors but actually broke it; the electoral revolt of many workers and peasants turning away from a PRI which inflicted such hardship on them; the unprecedented electoral outcome in 1988, in which the PRI admitted to only a bare majority of the vote and—for the first time—conceded both a handful of Senate seats and, in the summer of 1989, a governorship; and in general a civil society that has become more mobilized and ready to demand a more democratic regime. All these factors seem to suggest the inevitable erosion of a one-party system based on nego-

118

tiation and conciliation, a regime that was at once hegemonic and authoritarian.

DILEMMAS OF THE NEW POLITICAL PROJECT

In trying to understand the present crossroads, it may be helpful to focus on the political project of the de la Madrid "modernizers" within the government and the PRI and the challenge to that project presented by the sudden and unexpected rise of the FDN.

The government's commitment to economic restructuring was influential in the crystallization of a new project of political reform in the mid-1980s. Many of the traits of the existing one-party hegemonic regime were not consistent with the new economic orientation. The working class and the peasantry were no longer convenient bases of support in the context of the new economic orientation, which, with its emphasis on market mechanisms, competitiveness, efficiency, and privatization, left little room for policies protecting these sectors. At the same time, the middle class was a growing constituency that the modernizers wanted to target, but it was not effectively included in or organized by the Popular Sector within the PRI. This vulnerability was seen in the strength of urban support for opposition parties in 1988 and the losses by the PRI in three of the four largest cities in the country.*

Though some elements of the reform had been around for a long time, they came together in a new way in the second half of the 1980s to produce an overall project that could be seen as quite different. Past reforms of the electoral system, which had increased opposition representation in the Chamber of Deputies, seemed primarily aimed at perpetuating the existing system by neutralizing and/or coopting the opposition. As long as this goal was achieved and the one-party regime remained in place, a failure to implement proposed internal reforms of the PRI was not crucial. In the 1980s, however, the beginnings of a new political project which accompanied the commitment to economic restructuring envisioned a number of changes, although it did not foresee a loss of power by the

*The FDN won in Mexico City and the PAN in Guadalajara and Ciudad Juárez. The PRI won only in Monterrey.

PRI. The new political project can be analyzed in terms of three interrelated changes—in the PRI's constituency, in the nature of the regime, and in the role of the party in the reformed regime.

The first was a change in the constituency of the PRI. Corresponding to the new direction of economic policy toward "rationalization" and the free market was a need to establish greater state autonomy from sectors the state had been protecting through populist policies. The state alliance with labor and the peasantry became too costly in the context of the commitment to economic restructuring, and it now seemed outdated. The modernizers were no longer willing to protect groups from the market in the same way, and, as many PRI militants emphasized, the demographic changes that had made Mexico a more urban and middle-class society came to be seen as making obsolete the PRI's traditional constituency and its "overreliance" on labor and peasant support. At the very least, the modernizers envisioned that the terms of that alliance would be substantially changed and the party would be more centrally based in the growing urban middle classes.

Second was a move toward a more competitive regime and a change in the basis of legitimacy of the regime. Since 1917 the Mexican hegemonic regime had appealed primarily to a revolutionary legitimacy, and the underlying political myth (Lasswell and Kaplan 1950) was that the PRI represented the will of the people by embracing the coalition of the "revolutionary family." The symbolic or ideological resources of the regime that helped hold this coalition together were supplemented by material distributions through public policy. In David Easton's (1965: 267ff.) terms, the hegemonic regime was sustained by both diffuse and specific support. However, the capacity of a government based on PRI dominance to elicit both of these sources of support had been eroding. A generation had passed since the Revolution, which no longer evoked the same response sixty or seventy years later. More than the passing of years, however, the appeal to revolutionary symbols was undermined by the government's continuing and probably increasing political marginalization of the "revolutionary" classes—precisely those sectors that were supposedly "in" the coalition as against those that were supposedly "out." Compounding the erosion of the revolutionary claim was the growing inability or unwillingness of the government to buy support through specific policies, particularly with the economic crisis in the 1980s. As noted, a democratic claim to legitimacy had always been a component of the Mexican political myth—as seen, for instance, in the embarrassment of the government when one-party dominance had become "excessive" in the 1950s (prompting the introduction of the party deputy system), and in 1976, when López Portillo ran unopposed—but the democratic claim had always been subordinate to the revolutionary claim. A central part of the modernizers' project, then, was a change from a revolutionary to a democratic basis of legitimacy.

A precursor of the change in regime was the 1977 political reform. The reform can be seen as a recognition that the PRI no longer represented a coalition of the whole. Rather, many groups and tendencies in society were left out of the official channels of participation, as seen both in the number of unregistered parties that had been formed and in the high level of electoral abstention, which rose to a third or more of the electorate. New channels outside the PRI would have to be established. The Electoral Commission recognized that the myth of the PRI as all-inclusive had become dysfunctional and actually threatened the system rather than perpetuated its hegemony (Newell and Rubio 1984: 205).

In addition to its potentially greater effectiveness than a discredited revolutionary claim, the democratic legitimacy of a competitive regime would have a number of advantages from the point of view of the PRI modernizers. It would serve the function of past political reforms in Mexico: by including the opposition it would enhance stability and broad system support. Moreover, it would be consistent with the attempt to change the constituency of the PRI. It would provide a basis for loosening the alliance with labor, decreasing its influence, and leaving it with fewer claims on policy. Not only would labor lose its ideologically privileged status, but labor candidates for elected positions would no longer be protected from competition. The effect of competition was clearly seen in the 1988 elections, when eighteen of labor's sixty-six candidates (including some of the major figures within the labor movement) lost to opposition parties (Gómez and Klesner 1988: 7; Vásquez Rubio 1988: 8). Democracy would also have special appeal to the urban middle class, whose support the PRI wanted to attract; this class was not particularly open to revolutionary symbols nor effectively included in the symbolism of the revolutionary coalition. Finally, greater competitiveness and a democratic basis of legitimacy would be consistent with the economic project and the need to secure the cooperation of a skittish private sector, which frequently responded to uncertainty with capital flight. The change to democratic legitimacy could reassure the business community, which had always opposed labor's preeminent position even symbolically. (As noted, a proposal in 1978 to label the PRI "the workers' party" had been vigorously opposed.) In addition, the change might be seen as opening up the decision-making process in a welcome way, particularly since it was the pull of populist and labor pressures that was seen by the business community as responsible for erratic and unacceptable policies such as the bank nationalization.

The third change was from a coalitional party to an electoral, competitive party and from a dominant party to a majority party in a more open, competitive regime. The change foreseen here put a premium on internal party reform. A more open political process within the PRI was necessary to revitalize the party's internal life, enhance its capacity to choose good candidates, and thus enable it to win in clean, more competitive elections. Such reform would allow the party to maintain a majority political position through a more open process of reaching its supporters rather than through a largely hidden process of conciliation and bargaining with the top leaders of the organized sectors. Thus it was not a reform that would be incompatible with decreasing the influence of the party's sectors and shifting the support base of the party.

The crux of the government project that emerged in the mid-1980s, then, was a move from a one-party-dominant, hegemonic system based on revolutionary legitimacy, a "coalition of the whole" in which labor had a central role, and negotiation and conciliation within the revolutionary family, toward a majority party system more firmly rooted in the middle class and based on democratic legitimacy and on more open, political competition in which minority opposition parties would get a fair chance in clean elections. With respect to both a more competitive regime and the internal procedures of the PRI, the modernizers' commitment could be interpreted as serious; these political changes could be seen as a concomitant of the program of economic liberalization. Yet the simultaneous commitment to the PRI as the majority party must be kept in mind. For many opposition groups, the PRI has no place in a democratic

Mexico—as an "official" party it cannot oversee or participate in a genuine democratic process in which it competes fairly with other parties. Needless to say, this has not been the view of PRI activists. For example, Senator Roberto Madrazo, secretary of the PRI's National Executive Committee, stated,

> The democratization of the country without [the] PRI . . . is hardly feasible . . . [and] would be naive and bordering on the irresponsible (1989: 13).

The logic of the modernizers' project as it was emerging under de la Madrid seemed feasible until the last few months of the 1988 electoral campaign. Before then (as we have seen), the PAN still posed the greatest challenge to the PRI. Yet the challenge was limited, as the PAN demonstrated little potential for becoming a majority force on the national level. Furthermore, with the new economic orientation of the government, the modernizers within the PRI had little to fear from the PAN programmatically since the two parties were getting closer to each other on policy matters. Finally, the working class and the peasantry seemed to have few alternatives to supporting the PRI since the left had never made deep inroads among these groups. In consequence, with the new project it could be argued that the electoral support of the popular sectors would be largely maintained, but the state-labor and state-peasantry alliance would be substantially loosened and at least partially disarticulated, as was necessary from the perspective of economic liberalization. The government reform project was thus contingent on the particular political landscape that existed up to the 1988 elections.

The success of the Cardenist movement threw a monkey wrench into this project. The FDN presented powerful opposition to the economic policies of the PRI and offered an alternative that was more familiar to and more popular among the Mexican mass constituencies. In other words, it gave the traditional constituency groups of the PRI an attractive alternative. As a neo-Cardenist opposition movement, it was able to make a successful appeal on the basis of both a revolutionary and a democratic source of legitimacy, while the PRI was having difficulty with both. The 1988 election showed that the FDN (unlike the PAN) became a serious challenger with the possibility of winning nationally—even the presidency. As Senator Madrazo suggested, the PRI conceived of itself as a party of the

progressive-center, interested in competing with "incompatible" opponents which were "ideologically defined . . . [in terms of] right and
radical left," thus gaining a "margin toward the center" and reaping
"the psychological advantage with the voters of being the force that
conciliates the extremes" (1989: 14). In 1988, however, the FDN presented itself as a progressive force that could occupy the political
space traditionally claimed by the PRI. In many ways, it presented
itself as the "authentic" PRI—or as a kind of reembodiment of the
PRM: a national, populist movement that included the left and reproduced the PRM coalition, the heir to the Mexican Revolution that
was concerned with social justice, and the vehicle that was capable
of giving expression to the democratic yearnings of a newly awak-
ened political society. The emergence of the Cardenist opposition, in
short, meant that the PRI could no longer count on being the winner
in a new, more competitive, democratic regime as had appeared to
be the case prior to 1988. The 1988 elections therefore raised the
question of whether the government's reform project was being successfully challenged and derailed by the rise of opposition groups
with their own reform projects and whether reform from above was
being overtaken by reform from below.

The government's dilemma was complicated by the fact that
the modernizers' project did not represent the only position within
the PRI. The PRI had always represented a heterogeneous coalition,
but after 1986 the groups within it were no longer unified behind
the old economic policy combined with a one-party-dominant regime. Nor were they unified behind the government's new project
of economic and political liberalization. Rather, different groups
within the PRI occupied various positions with respect to economic
and political liberalization. These are represented in Table 1.

With respect to economic liberalization, one might recall the
distinction between técnicos and políticos. In what is undoubtedly
an oversimplification, one might say that the change in policy to
economic orthodoxy was generally associated with the técnicos, the
liberal modernizers epitomized in many ways by the recent presidents, de la Madrid and Salinas. Most of these were located in certain
ministries and state agencies (Bailey 1988: 67), but some of them were
also associated with party positions, such as Luis D. Colosio, the new
head of the PRI. Consistent with their backgrounds—their technical
training and their institutional connections—they put a high priority

Table 1

Currents Within the PRI

		Position on Political Liberalization	
		One-Party Hegemony	Political Opening
Position on Economic Liberalization	Moderated Change	Traditional PRI (caciques, sectors)	Progressive reformers (CD, CC[a], MCD[b])
	Orthodoxy	Other técnicos ?← – – – – –	Liberal modernizers (de la Madrid/ Salinas)

[a] = Corriente Crítica
[b] = Movimiento por el Cambio Democrático

on economic policy and rationalization. To summarize the previous discussion, these modernizers favored neo-orthodox, market-oriented economic policy representing a decisive break with the past. They argued that the model of import-substitution was spent and came to produce only inefficiencies in the form of high-cost production and an overly committed state in fiscal deficit. This faction within the PRI was growing over the last couple of decades and was given a big boost by the 1982 economic crisis and IMF conditionality.

Opposing the técnicos tended to be the políticos, who generally made their careers within the PRI and were more reluctant to change the economic policy which for so long gave them the leeway to distribute benefits to different constituencies as necessary to retain their political base. Many of these groups did not necessarily reject economic liberalization; rather they favored a slower, more cautious approach that would place a higher priority on reducing hardships than on making a forced and speedy economic adjustment. Included in this category were what might be called the progressive reformers—the heirs of Lázaro Cárdenas—as well as the traditional caciques (political bosses) and the sectoral interests of the party, whose positions were protected through government largess and intervention in the market.*

*Much has been made here and elsewhere of the técnico/político distinction, and a couple of points might be explicitly emphasized. It is essential to understand—and this is in many ways the point of our analysis—that when we refer

With respect to political liberalization, the alignment was somewhat different. Prior to 1988 the modernizers—or at least an important group of them generally associated with the president—favored the reform project outlined above. That is, they advocated a more open and competitive regime based on democratic legitimacy—though one in which the PRI would retain its position as the majority party—and they advocated party reform that to some extent would democratize or open the internal politics of the party. It would also seem that they sought to weaken or partly disarticulate the alliances

---

to the role of the técnicos, we are not dealing with economic policy-making in isolation from political policy-making, nor with a group of policy-makers who have no political instincts or insights and who are acting in the economic sphere in contradiction to the exigencies of the political arena. Quite the contrary, this analysis tries to show that a political project accompanies the economic project. Furthermore, the government's project of political reform and opening is not only a reaction to opposition (as was the case in the earlier reforms), but rather a positive effort to alter the political regime in order to make it compatible with the new economic direction. In addition, if the government's political reforms follow in part from its economic project, it is also the case that the economic project has not been formulated in a vacuum or simply in the course of technocratic training. It is probably not correct to see Mexican policy under técnico direction simply as approximating a "pure" economic approach, adopted by a "strong state" that has the capacity to ignore societal interests (unlike the more heterodox policy pursued in many other countries, where a weak state has had to give in to political demands). Rather, the Mexican state has relative strengths and vulnerabilities in its relations to different social sectors. Its strength in relation to labor has been widely noted, and much has been made of it here. In addition, however, as Kaufman (1988) has noted, Mexico's particularly orthodox, anti-labor, pro-business line should be understood with reference to the diminishing capacity of the Mexican state to thwart the demands of the private sector. The structural dependence of the capitalist state on the private sector means that the state's capacity to pursue policy is limited by the investment behavior of the private sector. In Mexico, given both the history of populist policies that have in the past been part of the coalition-tending behavior of the Mexican regime and the special links to the United States economy, the economy is particularly vulnerable to capital flight and a lack of business confidence. As Kaufman has suggested, "It was not 'economic rationality' alone which led the Mexicans to choose an orthodox approach. Rather, what was at stake was a choice between competing *political* logics" (1988: 103). The point is that the técnicos, despite the implication of the label that distinguishes them from the políticos, should not be seen as apolitical. Rather, they have their own political project, and they must be viewed as operating within and sensitive to a political regime and a political economic context which has given some sectors certain strengths relative to others.

that committed the state to the inefficiencies of protecting certain groups, especially labor and the weaker sectors of capital. The political reforms were consistent with this potential shift in the PRI's constituency. However, in the wake of the 1988 elections, it became clear that this position of the modernizers was contingent on the majority or clear plurality status of the PRI. A political opening and an appeal to a realigned constituency would contribute to the modernizers' objectives—providing the PRI could retain control over the government. This, of course, was the dilemma: the FDN showing in 1988 seemed to force a choice between political and economic liberalization. It raised the incentives for the modernizers either to abandon the course of political liberalization or to compromise their economic project in order to maintain the PRI's traditional constituency and base of support. It is the former that would presumably be seen as more tempting.

More unambiguously in favor of party and regime democratization and opening were the progressive reformers, who focused particularly on internal party reform. This current was marginalized within the party by the adoption of economic liberalism, but unlike the party sectors (see below), this wing would open the party to internal discussion and to greater grass-roots influence, making it less oligarchical and more open to progressive policy. Such a reform would strengthen the political position of the party. The Corriente Democrática advocated a limited internal reform when it was still within the PRI but was excluded from positions of power by the ascendancy of the de la Madrid/Salinas wing. Subsequently this reformist faction included the Corriente Crítica and the Movimiento por el Cambio Democrático (MCD), which took up the banner of reform but remained within the party. It also included some labor groups. These groups have been presented with the question of whether or not to stay in the party in the face of its inadequate reforms. The CD split demonstrated the unexpected possibility of success outside the party, but that success has not yet been consolidated. Though the Cardenists have been a pole of attraction, what is risked in opposition has also been clear.

The organized sectors of the PRI generally maintained a politically nonreformist stance for the same reasons the modernizers found political reform compatible with their goals: the sectors, like the political bosses, derived their position through negotiation and conciliation within the PRI; political competition and reform could weaken their position. Thus Fidel Velázquez has been a staunch opponent of political reform throughout his long career. As noted above, the issue is not one simply of the cooptation or corruption of top labor bosses. Despite the obvious and often noted disadvantages to labor in the one-party hegemonic system, the Mexican labor movement historically gained a number of benefits and did fairly well relative to other Latin American countries.* The alternative to negotiation and conciliation and the historic pattern of state-labor relations is not simply greater labor autonomy but—particularly in an era characterized by the global ascendancy of economic orthodoxy—the concomitant lack of existing levels of state protection that might leave labor potentially vulnerable with respect to such basics as the regulation of the right to strike, union rights, job security provisions, representation in the state, and a wide range of subsidies. With weak market power and relatively weak electoral power due simply to the size of the organized working class, labor has depended for its influence on organization in both political and economic arenas. From its point of view, this is the logic that makes sectoral organization within a dominant party attractive.

As the balance of power within the PRI has changed, as the modernizers have asserted their control and instituted their project, the scope for negotiation within a broad coalition has seemingly narrowed and a more oppositionist strategy may become less costly and more compelling. If prior to the 1980s the Mexican government in relative terms protected the material interests of labor and oversaw three decades of rising real wages, after 1982 it adopted a cheap labor policy. The new policy could be seen in the precipitous drop in real wages by nearly half—unparalleled in most other Latin

*The analysis of Jorge Salazar-Carrillo (1982) suggests that compared to the rest of Latin America, Mexico prior to the 1980s was a high-wage country. Measured in terms of both dollar equivalents and real wages in the textile and metallurgical sectors as well as overall manufacturing and specific occupations, and also adjusted for skill level and firm size, Mexican wages tended to be highest among those in eleven major Latin American countries. In terms of labor costs (including benefits as well as wages), Mexico generally slipped from first place but on almost all measures was above average. See also the assessment of Whitehead (n.d.: 24–25, 27), who maintains that compared to other Latin American countries Mexican labor enjoyed a number of benefits and, even by international standards, substantial autonomy and bargaining power.

American countries, also in the throes of severe debt crises.* It could also be seen in the wage levels of Mexico compared to those of the East Asian NICs, countries with which Mexico has been actively competing for investment in the export processing sector (as well as others). In 1980, the average manufacturing wage in Mexico was about three times higher than that in Korea and Taiwan; by 1987 it had become lower.† In addition to economic policy, the political context has also changed. As Jeffrey Frieden (1989: 32) has emphasized in his analysis of industrialists, the choice between coalitional and oppositionist forms of political activity, between negotiating concessions in exchange for political support and pressing demands from a position of opposition, depends on the likelihood of successful negotiations and the existence of allies in opposition. The calculations seemed to be changing for labor with the change of government economic policy and the sudden appearance in 1988 of a viable challenge to the PRI from the center-left.

FUTURE DIRECTIONS OF CHANGE

3 possibilities

In view of these dilemmas and ambiguities, what are the roads that Mexican politics might take? Three possibilities may be considered. One is that given the tensions within the PRI, the possibility of continued defections from the party, and the emergence of an impressive challenge from outside it, the PRI will either lose power or will be forced to share it, presumably with the Cárdenas forces. Another is that in order to forestall that eventuality, the government will back away from its political reform and maintain the one-party-dominant regime, but with greater recourse to fraud. Finally, the

lose or share power

more fraud to kp pwr

---

*See Gutiérrez Garza (1988: 146–54). The decline in real wages after 1982 and the comparison with other Latin American countries can be found in Roxborough (1989: 62).

†Calculations were made from data in U.S. Bureau of Labor Statistics (1990). According to these data, in 1975 Mexican manufacturing wages were 5.7 and 5.1 times those in Korea and Taiwan respectively. With the more rapid growth of real wages in Korea and Taiwan at the end of the 1970s, the gap narrowed, so that by 1979–81 (the last three years before the debt crisis and the plunge in Mexican wages), Mexican wages were about three times greater. By 1987 Mexican wages were 88 percent those of Korea and 72 percent those of Taiwan.

pol
(berlin)

③ government may persist and succeed in its project of controlled political liberalization.*

The first possibility signals the future success of the Partido de la Revolución Democrática (PRD—the new Cardenist party) or a more progressive coalition that could challenge the PRI. Cárdenas was, and seems to remain, extraordinarily popular. His personal attractiveness will be the key to the fate of the PRD in future elections. The capacity to translate his charismatic appeal into more institutionalized support remains an important question. On the one hand, the FDN in 1988 did unexpectedly well, exposed the great weakness of the PRI, and demonstrated its potential for winning outright, especially if effective electoral monitoring could be extended throughout the country. With this demonstration, its future ability to attract voters should be enhanced, for a vote for the PRD would no longer seem like a wasted vote. Workers apparently defected from the PRI in favor of the FDN in substantial numbers, and if the PRI maintains its current course, the "official" labor leadership may be increasingly tempted to do so as well. Similarly, progressive reformers within the PRI may be tempted to join the PRD in opposition.

On the other hand, the Cardenists had a difficult time forging a new party out of the electoral front of existing parties, the FDN. The satellite parties refused to join the new PRD, which was finally founded in May 1989 primarily on the basis of the Cardenist splinter from the PRI and the old PMS, which dissolved in order to form the new party. The prominence of the traditional left within the FDN gave its opponents the opportunity to attempt to discredit it for having an extreme, Marxist orientation, but in fact both the former components of the PRD explicitly rejected a socialist agenda in favor of (according to Cárdenas) a "nationalist program of the Mexican Revolution" (*New York Times*, 22 October 1988; *San Francisco Chronicle*, 24 May 1989).

A major issue dividing the FDN parties, both in the formation of the PRD and the relations among them since then, has been the question of "external" party cooperation. The satellite parties have been more inclined to see the PAN as the major antagonist while remaining more open to cooperation with the PRI. The PRD, in

---

*A fourth possibility is that the government would substantially modify, if not abandon, the turn to economic liberalism in order to renew the populist coalition. The government seems to have rejected this alternative.

contrast, has seen the PRI as the major opponent and has been willing to cooperate with the PAN in opposition to it. For instance, the PRD considered backing the PAN candidate for governor in the Baja California state elections in the summer of 1989, although in the end it opted for running its own candidate in order to preserve its alliance with the PPS and the PARM. By that time, however, a severe rupture had already occurred between the PRD and the PFCRN over the latter's cooperation with the PRI (*La Jornada*, 27 February 1989; *Latin American Weekly Report*, 13 and 20 April 1989). As relations between the PPS and the PRD drew closer in July 1989, a PRD deputy expressed a willingness to extend the alliance to the PARM but, again exposing the clash on this issue, "in no way to the PFCRN. . . . We would a million times prefer an alliance with the PAN than with [the PFCRN]" (cited in *La Jornada*, 28 July 1989).

Perhaps an even greater difficulty faced by the PRD is the government's potential for neutralizing the party as it has past schisms and opposition movements. The separate oppositions that erupted in the elections of 1940, 1946, and 1952 were each quickly absorbed by the PRI. After the 1988 election the government tried to defeat the Cardenist movement both through legalistic harass-ment (for instance, the PRD was legally forbidden to use the national tricolor as its party colors because the PRI also claimed them) and illegal muscle. The latter was seen most spectacularly in July 1989, when, according to virtually all non-PRI accounts, the government used blatant fraud to deny the PRD victory in local elections in Michoacán, the home state of Cárdenas, of which he had been governor and which in 1988 had voted for the FDN. Despite legal appeals and impressive protest mobilization on a number of levels— including the occupation of city halls and the blocking of highways and disruption of traffic—the government held firm and succeeded in dissipating the opposition's momentum, at least for the moment.

In addition to such coercive mechanisms, the PRI has tradition-ally had political resources for dealing with the opposition. For instance, the government has won popular approval through its ability to control inflation as a result of a continuation of the tripartite accord that it engineered with labor and capital. Further, as men-tioned, in the past the PRI had the capacity to ensure that splinter groups acted as satellite parties, playing a somewhat ambiguous game combining limited opposition with a more general pattern of cooperation. Though the 1988 elections demonstrated the potential for changing the balance between those two stances toward greater opposition, the PRI may have the resources to prolong the ambiguity and moderate the turn to outright opposition. In general, however, the economic reorientation combined with the new political dynamics may have affected the availability of these resources and the regime's ongoing capacity for successful conciliation and cooptation.

The possibility of greater reliance on more traditional political resources raises the second alternative: the continuation of a basically unreformed one-party-dominant system. Such an outcome would be a retreat for the PRI modernizers, both politically and (in order to sustain such a system) economically. The opposition evident in the 1988 elections provided a certain incentive for the PRI to retain its traditional constituencies and thereby seemed to increase the political resources and influence of what the modernizers have referred to as the "dinosaurs" within the party—the obsolete políticos, the anti-reformists who benefited from the old system and have been willing to engage in fraud to achieve PRI electoral victories.

As with the 1985 elections, two interpretations suggest somewhat different roles that the anti-reformers may have played in the 1988 elections. In the first, Salinas in the end retreated from his commitment to a fair count and hence turned to the dinosaurs, whose well-honed techniques for producing in the past a "clean sweep" of virtually all elected posts on the state and federal levels were necessary in 1988 to produce the barest of majorities. In the second, the Salinas forces continued to prefer a clean count and would have been satisfied with a mere plurality (few analysts would suggest the PRI had won the majority). However, in the disagreement and conflict that was responsible for suspending the count during the supposed computer breakdown, the Salinas reformers lost and the políticos prevailed.

By either account, the elections demonstrated that the anti-reformers in the PRI continued to wield considerable influence and that either because of the strength of the opposition or because of the new situation, Salinas would have a harder time than expected turning away from the old system and transforming the regime. In addition, with the urban and middle-class vote going heavily against the PRI, the elections showed that the PRI was more dependent than ever on its traditional constituencies—particularly the peasant vote in rural areas—further complicating the modernizing project and raising the stakes in a gamble on shifting the party's support base. Finally, despite government policy, the major labor organizations have continued to support the government in the traditional fashion and to provide a valuable resource. Particularly notable in this regard was the warm reception by the CTM and FSTSE of the debt accords signed by Mexico and its major creditors in July 1989 (*La Jornada*, 25 July 1989). These accords had important drawbacks for Mexico. They fell far short of what the government had earlier declared were its minimum requirements to renew growth; North American economists immediately announced their limitations; and they were greeted with criticism by Mexican opposition groups (particularly the PRD and PPS), who favored suspension of payments. Yet these labor organizations and Velázquez himself fell in line behind the government when it made a triumphal show of the accords. Despite this support, as the sexenio has worn on, Salinas has seemed increasingly committed to economic liberalization and hence to a policy which leaves little room for a continuing state-labor alliance along the old lines. Hence any labor strategy to remain in the governing coalition seems unlikely to meet with great success.

The third possibility, then, is the ultimate success of the PRI modernizers' project of economic and political liberalization. Precisely because of the first two trends—the unanticipated opposition and the consequent dependence of Salinas on the traditional constituencies and on relationships within the PRI—many expected that Salinas would have to moderate his reform project. During his first two years in the presidency, however, Salinas moved boldly to keep his project on track. The course followed in the opening years of Salinas's government will now be examined.

LIBERAL MODERNIZATION UNDER SALINAS

ECONOMIC LIBERALIZATION

With respect to economic policy, far from any retreat or modification, the Salinas government has intensified its commitment to economic restructuring and integration with the international economy as it has become more acutely aware of the changing organization of global production and patterns of trade and investment. Government policy has directly addressed the place of Mexico in the changing international division of labor, the development of a capacity in high-technology production, and the urgency of attracting foreign investment at a time when world attention has focused on the newly liberalizing countries of the Eastern bloc, to the potential neglect of Latin America.

Speeches by Salinas and government statements have repeatedly emphasized these themes. For instance, in May 1990 the Mexican Senate organized a national forum on Mexican trade (the Foro Nacional de Consulta sobre las Relaciones Comerciales de México con el Mundo), and Salinas's speech to that body emphasized how important it was for Mexico to adjust to the changing world economy. "We see an intense economic globalization of markets," he declared, "and the revolution in knowledge and technology makes all of us live, more than ever, a single universal history." In this context, Mexico must pursue "economic stabilization, debt renegotiation, fiscal reform, and structural change" as the "pillars" for integrating Mexico into the world economy. Furthermore, he saw international opening and cooperation as synonymous with "economic advance and political maturity." He denied that Mexico's integration and insertion into the international economy would lead to its "absorption." On the contrary, Mexico must "redouble its efforts" to "face the sharp international competition" precisely to "defend its sovereignty through economic modernization." Salinas stressed the changing economic and trade relations throughout the world, the formation of trading blocs, and the need for Mexico to define its relations with each—most importantly North America (the United States and Canada), the European Community, the Pacific Rim, and the Asociación Latinoamericana de Integración (ALADI) (Salinas 1990: 524–25). Similarly, emphasizing the main orientation of Mexican economic policy, the final report of the forum referred to the "necessity for Mexico to be incorporated into the new world economic currents and trade" for which "it is indispensable to increase productivity and economic competitiveness and to diversify exports" (Foro Nacional 1990: 540). Thus with the emphasis on international integration, increasing productivity and competitiveness are centrally important, and these are precisely the issues that make problematic the traditional one-party-dominant regime, constructed as it has been on a closely articulated alliance between the state and labor and based on a model that protects jobs, employment levels, and real wage increases in line with productivity growth.

The Salinas government's commitment to economic opening was seen most dramatically in the areas of the debt and free trade. As noted above, in July 1989, Mexico became the first Latin American country to sign a debt accord under the terms offered by the new Brady Plan. This plan contained guidelines for debt renegotiations which were supposed to offer some measure of relief in recognition of the need to promote economic growth after nearly a decade of stagnation. After months of hard bargaining, the government was unable to conclude a favorable bargain with international creditors. Despite a final agreement that in many ways represented a defeat for the Mexican government, Salinas declared that the Mexican debt crisis was over, thus continuing to put a high priority on good relations with its international creditors.

Even more breathtaking were the suddenness and speed with which in 1990 Salinas embarked on a free-trade agreement with the United States in a dramatic reversal of Mexican nationalism. Any treaty that may result from these negotiations would have the effect not only of institutionalizing the government's course of economic restructuring, but also in essence of removing much of this area of economic policy from the decision-making discretion of the Mexican government since many economic policies will be embodied in international treaty.*

As the Salinas government has not been deflected from its economic project, in many ways it has also continued to pursue its political project, despite the contradictions raised by the Cardenist electoral challenge. Although the rise of neo-Cardenism would seem to pressure the PRI to return to reliance on its labor base and reinvigorate the populist coalition, the government has persisted in loosening that alliance. Indeed to do otherwise would entail a retreat from the economic project. Somewhat more ambiguous has been the government's commitment to political liberalization. It will be argued that this political project has not been abandoned, but it has been more contorted by events.

*This use of a treaty to "lock in" the new policy orientation was directly acknowledged by a senior advisor to Salinas (see Campbell 1991: 23).

LABOR AND THE COALITIONAL BASIS OF THE REGIME

Welcome support for the debt agreement and a renewal of the tripartite accord notwithstanding, the new government quickly established a collision course with labor. Not only would a renewal of the state-labor relationship mediated through the PRI contradict the economic project, but the 1988 elections showed that the old-style coalition was no longer functional because they raised a question about the ability of labor leaders to deliver the vote to the PRI as they had in the past (Castañeda 1989b).

The attack of the Salinas government on labor has been presented as an attack on bossism and corruption in unions with the declared goal of democratizing the unions as part of the larger project of political liberalization. In evaluating this position, one must keep in mind the double-edged nature of liberalization and the way in which many groups in Latin America have favored "democratization" of unions as a way of reshaping and weakening the labor movement. In Brazil in both the mid-1930s and mid-1940s, for instance, liberals sought to decorporatize unions as a way of weakening them, and their attempts met with the opposition of organized labor (Collier and Collier 1991: ch. 5). Similarly in Argentina, the democratization of unions was attempted not only by President Raúl Alfonsín in the 1980s, but also by the repressive military government in the 1970s, in both instances as a way of weakening Peronism and the influence of labor (Munck 1990).

In any case, the nature of the attack on labor bosses indicates that, despite the rhetoric, the policy of the Salinas government has not in fact focused on cleaning up the corrupt unions and establishing a form of unionism that is closer to and more representative of the grass roots. Rather it has been aimed at eliminating sources of opposition to the government's liberal economic trajectory. One can see this in three major episodes of state-labor conflict which erupted during Salinas's first year as president.

The first episode occurred as a result of a government initiative in the opening days of the new sexenio and seemed intended to set the tone of state-labor relations during the Salinas presidency. It provided a clear signal that Salinas would not allow unions to stand in the way of economic restructuring and that he would not hesitate to attack any union, no matter how powerful, that did. The union in question was indeed strong: the oilworkers' union. Long headed by one of the country's most powerful labor bosses (Joaquín Hernández Galicia, known as "La Quina"), it had come to play a very influential role in the country's most important export sector; to control a vast multimillion dollar business empire that included factories, farms and ranches, and a range of retail establishments; and to negotiate relatively high wages and other benefits for its members.

Barely a month after occupying the presidency amid widespread anticipation of his political weakness and speculation that he might become dependent on the traditional PRI constituencies, Salinas moved against this union in a bold and startling manner. A military raid was conducted against the home of La Quina in which troops assaulted his house with rocket launchers and automatic weapons (*New York Times*, 12 January 1989). Hernández Galicia was arrested on charges of illegal arms possession; twenty other union leaders were arrested at the same time and another fifty or so the next day.

The attack on the union leadership represented the latest round in an ongoing conflict between Salinas and La Quina that, as we saw, dated to the previous sexenio, when Salinas, in his capacity as minister of budget and planning, had tried to incorporate the oil sector within the more general plans to increase economic efficiency and reduce state ownership. Following that initial salvo, Salinas had become the PRI candidate for president, and Hernández had, not too discreetly, supported Cárdenas, whose father had nationalized Mexican petroleum and introduced worker management in the industry. In the 1988 elections, the FDN did well in the areas with large concentrations of oil workers (*Proceso*, 25 July 1988; Vásquez Rubio 1988: 8; Whitehead n.d.: n. 19). After the elections, La Quina, seeking concessions for the oilworkers, had reportedly threatened to withhold from Salinas the support of union deputies in the Electoral College, where Salinas did not enjoy a large majority (*New York Times*, 12 January 1989, p. A6). The following October, tensions again flared when those deputies broke with the party and brought charges of corruption against the head of PEMEX.

The raid and arrests that capped this conflict with the petroleum union were the most dramatic clash between old and new models of state-labor relations. Salinas wanted to restructure the petroleum industry, perhaps break it up, privatize part of it, increase efficiency in an enterprise known for its inefficiency, and cut back the work force. In this, old-style unionism was a barrier. The union leadership was notoriously corrupt and employed gangster tactics to quash dissent, tactics that went as far as assassination. But the union delivered to its membership, winning favorable wages and contracts, keeping employment high through featherbedding, and generally preventing flexibility or change that would adversely affect the union or undercut the comfortable arrangements it had been able to work out in exchange for political support and substantial labor peace. In addition, as mentioned, the union was no longer politically reliable.

In arresting La Quina, the government claimed to be moving against a criminal, corrupt, and authoritarian union leadership. As noted, however, this move was at once against charro unionism and against the power of organized labor. The ambiguities made the incident a difficult one for dissident labor and political groups such as the FDN, most of which found themselves in the uncomfortable position of rallying to the defense of La Quina against the government's attack on union power. As the *New York Times* reported, the move was "seen as an unmistakable message that Mexico's new President intends to curb the power that unions have traditionally wielded" (12 January 1989).

This scenario contrasted with government actions toward the teachers' union, which was at the center of the second episode of state-labor conflict about two months later. In this case a strong dissident movement within the union existed in opposition to the leadership of Carlos Jonguitud Barrios, who, as a cooperative member of the PRI, had become a senator. Jonguitud was also a notorious union boss and was compared to La Quina even by groups within the PRI.

Stoppages in the first months of 1989 culminated in a strike called by a dissident reformist group within the union. Half a million teachers (perhaps half the union membership) throughout the country struck for higher pay and union democratization. Initially the government resisted giving in to the demands, declaring the strike illegal. The context in which the government finally relented and removed Jonguitud and the secretary general of the union was telling: not only was this a moment of particular mass pressure and dissident strength, but also the government viewed a change of leadership as consistent with the reform in education it favored

(Cook 1990). It is also interesting that the new secretary general was a protégé of Jonguitud's. The lesson to be derived from the episodes involving the oilworkers and the teachers is that the government was less hesitant to move against union bosses if they were not politically loyal and if they were seen as obstacles to government plans to restructure the particular sector. Put another way, union democracy was not an end but merely a means that could be employed to achieve the government's political and organizational or restructuring goals.

Another consequence of the teachers' strike may be noted. Confronted with a massive mobilization, the government in the end agreed to a 25 percent wage increase, a settlement out of line with the wage policy increase of about 10 percent (the minimum wage was increased 8 percent) and one it was not willing to extend to other workers. Nevertheless, this settlement became the basis of demands by other labor groups, and labor-state relations further deteriorated when the conflict that followed led to a head-on collision. For instance, in May 1989, 23,000 bus drivers in Mexico City demanded at a minimum the same 25 percent wage adjustment. The government, however, refused to be deflected from its economic policy in order to attend to its historic alliance with labor and fired the strikers (*Latin American Weekly Report*, 18 May 1989).

A further rupturing of the state-labor alliance took place in August 1989, when the union at the state-owned Cananea copper mine announced the intent to strike for improved wages and benefits when worker contracts expired at the end of the month. The government used the occasion to announce the bankruptcy and closing of the mine, thereby eliminating the jobs of nearly 4,000 workers.

Starting in the de la Madrid presidency, the government had tried to sell the mine to private owners. A deal was worked out in 1988, but it fell through partly because the necessary financing was not in the end available, but partly also because the union opposed the sale and the purported intention to reduce the labor force (*Latin American Weekly Report*, 7 September 1989). According to Mexican bankers and mining analysts, subsequent attempts to privatize the mine also failed because of "the extremely generous terms of labor agreements" that had been negotiated since the mine became state-owned in 1971 (*New York Times*, 30 August 1989). In August 1989, with the opening bargaining position of the workers amounting to a 330 percent increase in labor costs, the government took the opportunity to pursue its plan to reorganize the mine, seeking to achieve the conditions under which the mine could become more efficient and competitive and could reopen under private ownership with a reduced work force and more flexible labor contract. This action obviously had political costs, particularly at a mine which for historical reasons was an important symbol of the Mexican Revolution, working-class protest, and resistance to foreign domination. Cárdenas called it a "clear aggression against workers." It amounted to a statement about the government's political priorities and the salience of its economic project. According to the *New York Times*,

> a Government official said Mr. Salinas was well aware of the political symbolism surrounding Cananea and knew his decision to shut the mine would be unpopular and politically damaging. But the official said, the president is determined to pursue his plans to modernize the Mexican economy (30 August 1989).

This case provides another example of the incompatibility of traditional state-labor relations with economic liberalization and of the government's willingness to risk the alliance with labor in order to pursue its new economic policies. The same pattern could be seen in the government's $700 million project to modernize the state steel plants. In June 1989, in negotiations over a financing package with the IMF, the World Bank, and the Export-Import Bank of Japan, the government agreed to reduce the steel industry work force by 20 percent. This was part of a more general commitment, stated explicitly by the government in negotiations with the IMF, that Mexico would streamline and restructure state enterprises and improve their financial position (*New York Times*, 22 June 1989).

The above examples show that in his first two years as president, Salinas did not place high priority on patching over the cracks that had emerged in the traditional state-labor coalition. Certainly a concern with maintaining labor support did not interfere with his commitment to industrial restructuring along the lines of economic efficiency. Indeed his moves against union bosses occurred precisely when those bosses became obstacles to the government policy of restructuring that sector. The upshot was a continual deterioration in state-labor relations. A decisive rupture has not occurred, but it seems clear that government wants to effect a new relationship with labor more in line with the new economic orientation. Talk of the "new unionism" aside, the government has not yet effectuated any new model, but change may come more gradually and in connection as well with two events: the inevitable change in union leadership as labor bosses such as La Quina are removed and Velázquez enters his nineties, and the anticipated reform of the labor law, through which the government may attempt to alter the existing level of state protection of labor in line with the turn to economic liberalization.

POLITICAL LIBERALIZATION

If the Salinas government has been firm in its commitment to economic liberalization, it has also attempted to sustain its project of political liberalization, but in the new context it has done so in a number of contradictory ways. On the one hand, the government's policy of political opening and regime liberalization can be seen in the analyses by PRI militants that envision a new stage of democracy in Mexico. For instance, José Carreño Carlón, secretary of ideology of the PRI, distinguished three developmental stages. The first stage, *caudillismo*, consolidated the power of the victors in the Revolution; it was superseded by a second stage, *presidencialismo*, which resolved the issue of presidential turnover and established civilian control, but which, with the virtual monopolization of power by the PRI, maintained the Mexican electoral system in a state of "backwardness or underdevelopment." In the late 1980s, Carreño Carlón argued, Mexico entered a third stage, democratization, urgently demanded by the electorate; this stage would introduce political competition, a better balance between the executive and legislative branches of government, and an open process of decision-making (Carreño Carlón 1988). On the other hand, as mentioned, the government's commitment to political liberalization seemed contingent on its ability to guarantee PRI control of the national government. Salinas made this clear at the beginning of his presidency. In March 1989 he stated that the PRI "aspires to go on being a strong party, in order to prevent a slide toward a parliamentarian regime whose fragility would negate any possibility of efficacy, and would end in *des-gobierno* by minorities" (*Latin American Weekly Report*, 16 March 1989). Reflecting the dilemma in which the PRI modernizers have found themselves since the 1988 elections, the attempt to provide for these two often contradictory goals has taken various, sometimes self-negating forms, which can be seen in a new electoral law, a new internal party reform, and a resort to strong-arm measures to assure outcomes favorable to the PRI.

Electoral Reform. The new electoral law began to take shape less than a year after Salinas was inaugurated, and final action on it was completed in August 1990. Just as the 1986 electoral reform seemed to respond to the challenge presented by the PAN and seemed to open the political system while basically protecting the PRI's leading position, so the new law was a response to the electoral challenge presented in 1988. Similarly, its logic revealed a leadership desirous of protecting the interests of the PRI while accepting a more competitive regime. If the 1986 law seemed geared to the establishment of a one-and-a-half party system (accepting the PAN as an important competitor but one unlikely to win a national majority), the new law seemed designed around a possible three-party system.

Two provisions were particularly important. First, the new law maintained the 1986 governability clause, giving the largest party an absolute majority in the Chamber of Deputies, but for the first time it set a minimum on the percent of the vote such a party must win in the election to be eligible. The 1986 law set no minimum: presumably a party with 25 percent or less of the vote could be allocated a majority of seats in the Chamber so long as it was the leading party. The new law stipulated that only a party winning at least 35 percent would be eligible for these "unearned" seats.* Second, the largest party would also be given two seats for every percent of the vote it won above 35 percent (the "over-overrepresentation" clause). Parties winning 60 percent or more would not be eligible for these additional

---

*While many analysts have been struck by the explicit way in which the law afforded a governing majority to a party—presumably a weakened PRI—with as little as 35 percent of the vote, the innovation of this law was in fact that it actually raised—or provided—a minimum national vote for a party to be entitled to this form of overrepresentation. As we shall see, this innovation is interesting in that it revealed a new electoral logic or calculation.

seats. A party winning between 60 and 70 percent of the vote would be allocated PR seats so that its total number would equal its overall percent of the vote. The maximum a single party could hold remained 70 percent of the seats.

The implications of these changes are interesting. In general, the new law continued to set the stage for a majority-party rather than a dominant-party system. So long as a party could win at least 35 percent of the vote, it would achieve a majority in the Chamber of between 50 percent (plus one seat) and 70 percent. But this feature was not new. What was new was what happened if the largest party failed to get 35 percent of the vote. Over 35 percent, the electoral system would distort the allocation of seats in favor of the largest party: the lower the percent of the vote up to 60 percent, the larger the distortion. Under 35 percent, however, the distortion would be eliminated and the system would become one of proportional representation.* It is interesting to contemplate a three-party system with the vote more or less evenly divided and no party winning 35 percent. If under these circumstances the PRI was not the largest vote-getter, the party that was would not benefit from the gov-

*As a party improves its percent of the vote from 35 to 60 percent, the electoral system moves from its highest point of distortion in the distribution of seats relative to percent of vote toward proportional representation. There are two principles of distortion. Principle 1 is the governability clause, which allocates seats necessary for forming a majority. In the extreme case, if we assume that a party winning only the necessary minimum of 35 percent also wins at least 35 percent (or 105) of the majority seats, then a maximum of 146 PR seats will be allocated to that party to reach the bare majority of 251 total seats. Principle 2 is the "over-overrepresentation" clause, which allocates 2 seats to the largest party for every one percentage point of its vote over 35 percent up to 60 percent. At 35 percent, a party would not receive any seats according to this provision, and at 60 percent it would receive the maximum number, or 50. Thus according to Principle 1, the distortion decreases from a maximum of 146 seats to zero as the percent of the vote increases from 35 to 60 percent. According to Principle 2, the distortion increases from zero to 50 seats with the same increase in the vote. In this way, Principle 2 "restores" some of the overrepresentation "lost" from Principle 1 as a party approaches 60 percent of the vote. Nevertheless, because of the difference in magnitude, the overall distortion would decrease as per Principle 1 as a party goes from 35 to 60 percent. All in all, the electoral system is a PR system if the largest party has under 35 percent; at 35 percent it reaches its maximum distortion in favor of the largest party, with that distortion decreasing toward PR at 60 percent; finally, at over 70 percent it distorts in favor of opposition parties by declaring that a maximum of 70 percent of the seats can be held by any single party.

[handwritten margin note at top: PRD + PAN very unlikely that they cld from a coaltn v. PRI. So if PRI not dominant it could make a coaltn w/ one of the 2.]

ernability provision. Quite the contrary: the PRI would be in a favorable position to bloc that party through the formation of a coalition. This could have special benefits for the PRI since the PRD and the PAN would be unlikely to form a governing coalition, especially on matters of economic policy. In other words, so long as the PRI remained the largest party and could win at least 35 percent of the vote, the new law maximized its victory. If the PRI lost in a close vote divided among three parties, the law minimized the loss and might even allow the PRI to overcome it through what might be its special pivotal position in forming coalitions.*

The new electoral system could thus be seen in light of the dual government strategy. On the one hand, it included provisions which protected the PRI and its capacity to form a governing majority. On the other, it had provisions for a more open political system in which the representation of opposition parties was increased. If the 1986 law seemed to support a change in the status of the PRI from a dominant to a majority party, the new law seemed to allow the PRI to rely on only a plurality. This more competitive context put a premium on the ability of the PRI to function as a successful electoral organization, a genuinely popular party that could stand up to the heightened electoral competition. Therefore, a second element in the government's political project was another attempt at internal party reform, which became essential to the survival of the PRI as a vote-getting institution in a more competitive context.

[handwritten margin note: II.]

Party Reform. A new effort at party reform followed the same logic as the prior one under de la Madrid. It was an attempt both to make the party competitive and to change its coalitional basis in line with the new economic project and changes in Mexican society. Since the party took its basic organizational form in the 1930s, Mexico has been transformed from a rural to an urban society. Its fastest growing urban groups have not been embraced by the party

*A similar result would obtain if the PRI remained the largest party but failed to win 35 percent. In this case, of course, it could not benefit from the governability clause, but again would presumably be privileged in forming a governing coalition with another party. Ironically, the condition under which the new law left the PRI most vulnerable was precisely the outcome that the PRD claimed for 1988—i.e., one of the three parties (the PAN in 1988) failed to pull "its" third of the vote, and another (the PRD) won a plurality of over 35 percent. In this case, the opposition, not the PRI, would benefit from the distortions built into the law.

sectors and demand some other mechanism of political participation. These groups include both the middle class and the urban informal sector. The reform was conceived as a response to these social and demographic changes—as a way to strengthen party structures most relevant to the new groups and weaken those most relevant to the traditional constituencies. It moved toward a transformation of a hierarchical, bureaucratized, corporate party directed by political bosses ("dinosaurs") to a modern, democratic, popular party with a reinvigorated territorial organization at the base and less emphasis on the sectoral organizations.

Party renovation, modernization, and democratization were forcefully pronounced high on the agenda in speeches at the March 1989 celebration of the sixtieth anniversary of the PRI. A new plan was adopted early in the sexenio. The first step was a PRI "census" to identify PRI members and form the basis for internal democratization. At the core of the territorial (as opposed to sectoral) structure of the party were 45,811 sectional committees. According to PRI documents, as of mid-October 1989 party members had elected the leadership of more than half of these. Similarly, somewhat over half of the 2,383 municipal party committees had newly elected leaders. In 7 states, the party chose state and local candidates by one of two methods: 1) secret vote of delegates democratically elected by the territorial and sectoral structures, or 2) primary election. In elections during 1989, the party claimed great success as a result of this internal renewal process: in 9 states where elections were held, it lost overall in only one, winning *all* elected posts in 4 and winning a majority (usually overwhelming) in 4 others. In 7 states for which the PRI made data readily available, the party recaptured much of the vote it had lost in 1988 (Madrazo 1989: 18–23; PRI 1989). With the initiation of this reform, the party began to make the claim of democratic legitimacy, as evidenced in the teams of PRI leaders sent to deliver the message to U.S. universities. Elections in 1990 similarly showed the PRI improving on its 1988 record and explaining its renewed popularity with reference to party reform and the rejuvenation of its base organizations, though in many of these elections the opposition brought charges of electoral fraud. As we shall see below, fraud remained an instrument of electoral victory, but it nevertheless seems that the PRI regained substantial popularity, particularly in off-year elections, when the opposition could not rely on the coattails of an attractive presidential candidate. However, the role of party reform in producing these positive outcomes is far from clear. The reforms are still getting underway, studies are not yet available to indicate how the reforms have proceeded on the ground or how sectoral interests have—or have not—been accommodated, and past history preaches caution, as earlier reforms have been undermined.

The problematic nature of party reform could be seen in a second component of the reform, which was to occur in the context of the Fourteenth National Assembly of the PRI, convoked in the fall of 1990. Delegates were to be democratically chosen, and the assembly had the role of formalizing the reorientation and "modernization" of the party. On a rhetorical level, the party rededicated itself to certain traditional symbols of the Revolution, social justice, and national sovereignty, at the same time that it emphasized some new themes of pluralism, democracy, human rights, the environment, and gender equality. It went on record as adopting a "new mentality" in line with the "new political thinking in the world today" (*La Jornada*, 2 September 1990).

Beyond rhetoric and the adoption of principles, however, the assembly proved less successful in introducing democratic processes, and internal strains and opposition over this issue developed within the party. Two dissident factions, the Corriente Crítica and the MCD, skeptical from the beginning, were particularly critical of the procedures adopted, both for electing delegates to the assembly and for electing party leaders within the assembly. They charged that the PRI had not in fact lived up to its announced intention to democratize the party: base level party organizations remained open to manipulation, undemocratic state governors continued to wield power within the party, most of the delegates were handpicked by party leaders rather than selected by the base organizations, and decisions had been made by the leadership beforehand and merely ratified by the assembly (*Proceso*, 26 February 1990; *Latin American Regional Report*, 27 September 1990). In the end, the MCD held a Day of Protest against the failure to implement reforms, and the leader of the Corriente Crítica, Rodolfo González Guevarra, left the PRI after forty-four years in the party (*Latin American Regional Report*, 1 November 1990).

In the first half of 1991, the course of party reform seemed to flounder once again, when the time came to choose candidates for the August elections for the National Congress and some state governors. The selection process seemed to retain the traditional pattern of top-down *dedazo* (designation; literally, "fingering") by central party leaders and state governors, differing only in the way in which the party labeled it. This time the party followed the "fast track" and named lists of "unity candidates."

These developments highlight the many ambiguities and contradictions in the government project of party reform, parallel to those regarding electoral reform. The government sought to create a more effective party, capable of attracting the votes needed to stay in power, and at the same time to shift the coalitional basis of the party away from its traditional constituencies (organized in the party sectors) toward a more middle-class, and perhaps informal-sector, constituency that would take part in the territorial rather than the sectoral organizations of the party. However, the government also had two other goals that it sought to coordinate with this one: preventing a defection by the traditional constituencies to, for instance, the PRD, and boosting support for its neo-liberal economic policies.

On the one hand, the reform project was seen as a way to enhance the popularity of the PRI and create a new constituency more consistent with the neo-liberal economic policies; on the other hand, the party could less afford to alienate its labor and peasant base completely, now that an attractive alternative existed, lest it risk growing opposition to its economic policies. This dilemma can be seen in the still unresolved issue of how and how far to decorporatize the party and to move from a sectoral to a territorial organization. Party democratization would weaken the political influence of unions (and indeed, once again the CTM's Velázquez had led the opposition). Yet it was not clear that the PRI could afford to forego labor support and cooperation. The government seemed to be searching for a solution in the still vague notion of a "new unionism." The new model of democratic unionism would somehow be consistent with modifying the old-style underpinnings of the coalition with labor while retaining labor's electoral support and cooperation in both macro and micro policy. On the macro level, since 1988 anti-inflation policies have been based on a social pact between labor and the private sector which the government engineered in tripartite negotiations. Similarly, on the micro level, the government has held up as an exemplar the labor negotiations that accompanied the restructuring of the telephone industry and the preparation for its privatization. The capacity to forge cooperation and form social pacts has been a distinctive trait of the Mexican regime and the old pattern of state-labor relations. It will be interesting to see if that capacity can be retained in the new economic and political context and if it is indeed consistent with the new unionism. Given these dilemmas, the party reform project remained uncertain.

III .

Political Coercion. It may be precisely because of the ambiguities and contradictions surrounding the new electoral system and the party reform project that the government has relied on coercion. Though on the one hand the use of coercion negates the liberalizing thrust of the political modernization goals, on the other hand, the government has resorted to authoritarian means to structure the party system along lines consistent with its vision of the future. Specifically, it seemed to be attempting to shape a party system similar to that which existed before mid-1987—that is, a party system in which a majority PRI found its greatest electoral challenge and opposition in a regionally based PAN, a system that, it was argued above, would give the PRI the scope to pursue political liberalization and loosen the close links with the labor movement without jeopardizing its control of the state. The rub, of course, was the PRD. Accordingly, the government seemed to be on a path to eliminate the PRD as an important force through intimidation, selective repression, and even assassination in order to make the country "safe" for democracy—or to make democracy safe for the PRI.

In this attempt to structure the political landscape, the government also relied on electoral fraud. It may be noted that at the same time the new electoral law seemed to provide the conditions under which the PRI could accept a new status as a mere plurality party, it failed to liberalize the institutions for the conduct and oversight of elections—and may even have been a step backward in this regard. The government's continued—or even tighter—control of the electoral machinery was perhaps the most retrograde feature of the new electoral law and probably the one that provoked the greatest opposition. The possibility of using this control to perpetrate electoral fraud as a last-ditch means of structuring the party system could be seen most dramatically in local elections held in the sum-

Table 2

Political Opposition Groups

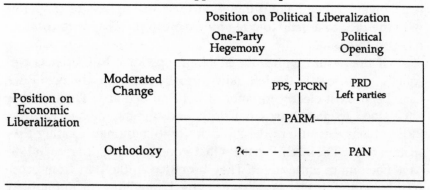

		Position on Political Liberalization	
		One-Party Hegemony	Political Opening
Position on Economic Liberalization	Moderated Change	PPS, PFCRN	PRD Left parties
		PARM	
	Orthodoxy	?← – – – – –	– – – – PAN

mer of 1989 in Baja California and Michoacán. In the former, the PRI ceded important victories to the PAN: two municipalities, eight majority seats in the Chamber of Deputies, and—an unprecedented concession—the governorship. In the latter, however, by virtually all accounts, the government resorted to electoral fraud to deny the PRD victory, despite the admission that even by the PRI's own reckoning the PRD had edged ahead of it in the popular vote (PRI 1989). Such a tactic had the advantage of complicating cooperation between the PRD and the PAN in defense of clean elections.

The question of inter-party cooperation again raised the issue of where different parties—or tendencies within parties—stood with respect to economic and political liberalization. Table 1 showed the positions of factions within the PRI on political and economic liberalization. Similarly Table 2 shows the positions of the opposition parties. Together they give some indication of the possibilities of both factionalization and compromise or cooperation. In terms of economic liberalization, the opposition groups have been split, as one might expect, along ideological lines: the PAN has favored a free-market orientation, whereas most of the parties that formed the FDN in 1982—the left-leaning satellite parties and the new PRD—as well as the leftist PRT to different degrees have opposed it, or at least would modify the implementation of the policy in order to ameliorate the social costs. The PAN, however, has been less united on the issue of political liberalization, as have been the parties that made up the FDN. As opposition parties, all tendencies within the PAN and the former FDN have favored some form of political opening as all have needed some room to operate; the more the electoral system provides for their increased representation, the better. However, they have differed on their willingness to cooperate with the PRI, to accede to a regime favoring the PRI, or to compromise on this issue.

Of the parties within the FDN, groups loyal to Cárdenas personally and those to the left, now formally united in the new PRD, have been most clearly in favor of political opening. These groups have stood to gain least from deals and understandings with the PRI, not least because of the PRI's desire to marginalize rather than sustain them. The satellite parties that stood behind Cárdenas in 1988 have been more ambivalent. They benefited in the past from cooperation with the PRI and have seemed unwilling to definitively forego that cooperation by formally joining the opposition PRD, despite their good showing in 1988. The source of their ambivalence is illustrated by the PARM, which, when confronted with the danger of losing its registration because of its poor showing, was rescued both by PRI protection and by its alliance with Cárdenas.

The PAN has also been in a dilemma. On the one hand, it has traditionally been the largest opposition force, the party that would reap the advantages of political liberalization. Yet the 1988 election demonstrated the distinct possibility that it was not the PAN but the Cardenists that might benefit most from political reform. The PAN thus seemed to be presented with the alternatives of an unreformed regime and PRI dominance versus a reformed regime and a Cardenist victory.

In the mid-1980s, the neo-panistas, or Clouthier wing, became influential in setting the tone of the PAN's less compromising, more confrontational position on political liberalization. However, the 1988 elections may have altered the balance of power within the party and moderated PAN opposition, potentially disposing it toward some type of cooperation with the PRI, for those elections demonstrated that the PAN probably did not have the potential to become a majority party—or perhaps even, without the aid of the PRI, the largest opposition party. Rather, that position was more likely to be occupied by a party whose economic policies the PAN regarded as even worse than those of the PRI.

The dilemma of the PAN led to an important split in the party over the new electoral law of 1989-90. A dissident wing maintained a more uncompromising position and, like the PRD, opposed the government outright throughout the nearly two years during which the legislation was before the Chamber of Deputies. However, the dominant wing of the PAN, headed by Luis Alvarez, led the party into negotiations and ultimately cooperation with the PRI in passing the reform.

Electoral reform

The electoral reform was enacted in two stages: the constitutional amendment of October 1989 and the new electoral code which implemented it in July 1990. In the first stage, a two-thirds majority was needed, and hence the PRI, with just over half the seats in the Chamber of Deputies, was dependent on the cooperation of other parties. Salinas was therefore willing to listen when the PAN presented "seven basic points" which it considered essential in the new law. After tough negotiations and maneuvering, the PAN agreed to support the draft amendment in exchange for a "letter of intent," pledged to by Salinas and PAN leaders, in which both accepted PAN suggestions as guidelines for future changes in drafting the code itself.

Though the amendment was passed on the basis of this cooperation, the PAN leadership was not able to bring the dissident wing of the party in line behind this vote. In the following months the rift in the party deepened, as the politics of the second stage developed. In November one-third of PAN delegates to a meeting of the party's National Council voted against the electoral reform (*Proceso*, 15 January 1990, p. 20). In February 1990 internal party elections returned Alvarez to the leadership, but the following month the PAN dissidents formed the Foro Doctrinario y Democrático (FDD), denouncing the leadership for "treason"—for betraying the principles of the PAN and abandoning the seven basic points. It warned the party against the illusion of sharing power with the PRI and against abandoning its principles and acquiescing in the continuation of what it had historically opposed—the corporatist control of the PRI machinery over the state. The dominant Alvarez faction, on the other hand, believed in the advisability of alliance with the PRI and argued that it wanted to consolidate gradual advances in the process of democratization (*Proceso*, 23 July 1990, pp. 14, 16, 21).

The position of the PRI with respect to the PAN was also interesting. Salinas seemed more willing to cooperate than did the party's legislative delegation. As negotiations over the code continued, debate raged within the PAN over whether it was shaping up as a reform or a counter-reform; as the vote neared, the party seemed to be joining the PRD in opposition. The Salinas government maintained a hardline position with respect to the changes referred to in the letter of intent. Unlike the constitutional amendment, the code required only a majority vote, which the PRI itself had. Nevertheless, the government felt it was politically useful for the code to pass with multiparty support. In the end, an agreement was reached and the government secured the PAN's cooperation. However, once again, one-third of the PAN delegates voted against the law, and the party emerged from the battle severely divided and debilitated (*Proceso*, 23 July 1990, p. 16).

The machinations surrounding the electoral law provide a good illustration of the fluidity of Mexican politics and the basis for political divisions and realignments. Particularly striking is the potential for cooperation between factions of the PRI and the PAN, both of which have shared an economic project of liberalization but have been caught off balance by the rise of the PRD with respect to their commitment to political liberalization. For both groups political liberalization has been attractive insofar as it advanced the liberal economic project. If instead political liberalization were to lead to the relative success of the PRD, empowering rather than marginalizing the populist constituencies and at the very least modifying the liberal economic project, then the possibility of cooperation would seem particularly great—either to retreat from political liberalization (as indicated, for example, in provisions of the electoral code which retained or even increased the PRI's control over the electoral machinery) or to form a new majority bloc which would allow political liberalization to proceed in a way that would produce a desirable outcome.

This, however, is not the only line of cooperation. The issues of political and economic liberalization have led to a series of dilemmas and hence to divisions among and within most political parties and groupings. In contrast to the old alliance pattern, the picture now is one of cross-cutting cleavages: PRI versus opposition groups; orthodox economic liberals versus those unwilling to bear the social costs; and uncompromising political reformers versus those willing to compromise. These cleavages define multiple groups, each with its own political-economic project, as well as many possibilities for cooperation. Indeed since 1988 Mexican politics has seemed particularly fluid, characterized by constant realignments rather than stable coalitions. The future will reflect the political struggles among the groups and the interactions among these projects.

Chapter 6

CONCLUSION: ECONOMIC AND POLITICAL
LIBERALIZATION

This analysis has considered Mexican politics within a critical juncture framework which focuses on periods of political reorientation when new structures and institutions are founded, often in response to major socioeconomic change. It described first the dynamics of a critical juncture earlier in this century that saw the institutionalization of a one-party-dominant inclusionary regime which derived its legitimacy and support from labor and the peasantry. In interpreting the current changes, the question could be asked if, in the context of the present period of socioeconomic change, Mexico has entered a new critical juncture involving a major political reorientation and change of regime. Are we witnessing limited reforms of the old regime or more fundamental alterations of the regime and of the revolutionary coalition based on worker and peasant support? If it is argued that throughout Latin America the nature of labor incorporation was an essential feature of the earlier critical juncture and labor's coalitional position was a crucial outcome, then in raising the question about the persistence of the Mexican regime and the possibility of a new critical juncture, the role of labor and its political position are of particular importance.

The critical juncture of the earlier incorporation period emerged in response to particular socioeconomic changes and correspondingly in a specific historical and economic context which made certain political coalitions possible. Many of these conditions have now changed. Evidence of economic transformations that might constitute the basis for a new critical juncture leading to a change in the structure of political coalitions and cleavages can be observed in many areas, both international and domestic. Indeed the international factors by themselves seem important enough to suggest the possibility of fundamental change, and they help account for the political transformations that were occurring not only in Mexico, but also in countries throughout the world in the 1980s. These global trends in the late twentieth century place new constraints on the state-labor coalition and produce new pressures for regime change.

At the most general level the present period is one of a major reorganization of capital on a global scale. National economies have become more closely integrated and interdependent with the expansion of world trade, including intra-firm transfers as multinational corporations (MNCs) have internationalized their production. A new international division of production has come about, with the rise of NICs as low-cost producers and suppliers of manufactured goods. Further, with the off-shoring of certain stages of production by MNCs, some Third World countries—including Mexico with its border industry—have participated in the new globalization by expanding the export assembly sector partly on the basis of cheap labor. The increasing integration has produced a new hegemony of economic orthodoxy, liberalism, and market ideologies that puts a premium on competitiveness and efficiency. The effects are seen in countries as diverse as the historically laissez-faire United States, the welfare state of Great Britain, and, most dramatically, the command economies of China, the Soviet Union, and Eastern Europe, as well as Latin America.

Far-reaching changes have also been occurring at the firm and sectoral level, where restructuring has been taking place. With the introduction of new technologies, based on the revolution in semiconductors, fordist patterns of assembly-line production have begun to give way in some sectors to more flexible forms of production. Work forces have been reduced, and in some industries new kinds of subcontracting arrangements are being implemented. Evidence in some countries is beginning to suggest that as this reorganization of work occurs, the system of industrial relations based on nationally organized unions may be superseded. While the introduction of such labor processes has been limited in countries like Mexico, their presence in a few key industries may become influential in setting the tone for the overall orientation of the industrial relations system.

There is no question that these social and economic changes have exerted pressure on the inclusionary one-party-dominant regime in Mexico and on labor's coalitional position. These factors are widely recognized in accounts of Mexican politics—both by professional analysts and by political actors. For instance, in explaining the PRI's new project of political reform, Senator Madrazo emphasized the centrality of the task of economic modernization and restructuring in light of changes in the international economy, referring to the "great world transformation" in which Mexico wants to become an "active participant" and must therefore "overcome the obstacles to be confronted in a highly competitive world" (Madrazo 1989: 10–11).

Other factors specifically affect Mexico as well as other Latin American countries and would also seem to be altering the coalitional logic and labor's place in it. Most obvious is the staggering debt burden, which erupted into a full-fledged crisis in 1982. Since then, economic policy, influenced by IMF conditionality, has produced low or negative economic growth, a period of net capital outflows, inflationary pressures, unemployment, a dramatic drop in real wages, and a declining standard of living. Also important are changing patterns of industrialization: the apparent stagnation of import-substituting industrialization and the consequent argument that a new model, typically involving export promotion, must be introduced, a model that again emphasizes efficiency and competitiveness. The removal of protectionist barriers to free trade and the new emphasis on exports have had important consequences for labor, often leading to a contraction of the labor force: some firms have not been able to adjust to international competition and have gone bankrupt; some have sought to achieve efficiency by laying off workers; some have sought to become competitive by adopting new (labor-saving) technologies. Finally, in the decades since the earlier critical juncture and the incorporation of labor, the social structure has been transformed with the growth of the middle class, the strengthening of the private sector, and rapid urbanization involving a declining peasantry and a growing urban informal sector.

In the 1980s, groups favoring a new neo-orthodox economic agenda have gained power and influence in Mexico. These include factions of the private sector outside the government. An illustration of the pressure such groups exert on the state-labor coalition is the call by private sector leaders of COPARMEX for the destruction of the CTM and the CROC (the two labor confederations closest to the government), based on the charge they were "prostituted by corruption and politicization" (Trejo Delarbre 1987: 60). Moreover, factions

within the government—the so-called modernizers, who have become increasingly influential in the economic ministries and in the
presidency itself—have also adopted this position. Given their ex-
pertise and general orientation, the modernizers put prime importance on the economic project of making the Mexican economy more
efficient, more competitive, and more integrated into the international economy, and they seem largely, though not exclusively, to
have constructed their political project around the goal of economic
restructuring.

The government's reorientation toward economic liberalism has
profound implications for the state-labor alliance which has been so
central to the Mexican regime since the incorporation period. If the
logic of the earlier critical juncture was conducive to the formation
of a state-labor alliance, the logic of the potential new critical juncture
points to the disarticulation of that alliance. The state-labor alliance
rested on the assumption of state protection of labor from an untram-
meled labor market. Such protection was a feature not only of radical
populism in the 1920s and 1930s, but also of the subsequent period
in which labor, though still included in the coalition, played a more
subordinate role. This protection was evident not primarily perhaps
with respect to high and continually rising wages, but with respect
to such things as wide-ranging subsidies on consumer goods and
housing, job security, fringe benefits, and worker representation on
labor boards and other state agencies. From the perspective of a
liberal economic agenda, however, the inefficiencies of that protection
became unacceptable, and the efficiencies presumably gained from
market discipline took on paramount importance.

On the other side of the political spectrum, reformist and leftist
groups, such as the PRD, the PRT, and dissident labor groups, find
the hardships inflicted by the new policies after 1982 unacceptable.
Yet they also favor severing the state-labor alliance, both because
that alliance has served as a vehicle for state control over labor,
limiting its ability to influence the new economic direction, and
because the alliance, achieved through the corporatist organization
of the PRI, has made it difficult for opposition parties to woo labor
successfully.

The official labor movement has become increasingly isolated
in its tenacious attachment to the old arrangements, fighting a rear-
guard action to maintain its position and prevent the PRI modern-

izers from distancing it from positions of influence. However, given the determination of the government to proceed with the new policies, even official labor must begin to question the advantages of its alliance with the state.

In a related manner, economic changes created the conditions under which diverse groups with quite contradictory goals came to favor a more open and competitive political regime. After 1982 the new economic policies spawned three different projects for political liberalization—either to advance or retard economic liberalization. The first, emerging by the early 1980s, was an opposition project mounted by the PAN and a group of newly militant businessmen who became politically active in the party. In the context of global economic changes and especially with the growing integration of the northern Mexican economy with that of the United States, they advocated liberal economic policies even more energetically and came to see a competitive political regime as necessary for successfully pressing their policy demands and subordinating the influence of labor.

The second project, developed after 1985, was that of the PRI itself. In part, it was an effort to deal with the political challenge presented by the newly militant PAN and the legitimacy crisis provoked by the government's use of electoral fraud. In this sense, the PRI's project of political liberalization was similar to previous political reforms that had increased the representation of opposition parties, while simultaneously shoring up the legitimacy of the PRI-dominated regime. This time, however, the changed economic context gave new meaning to the government's project. With the adoption of liberal economic policies, the PRI modernizers came to see the party's base of support in the popular sectors as problematic and outmoded. Political liberalization came to be viewed as a way of disarticulating the state-labor alliance and changing the social support base of the state.

The third project was that of the Cardenists, whose break with the PRI was in part a reaction to the government's abrupt change of economic policy. Though the Cardenists' move to overt opposition was a response to various developments, including internal politics within the party, the success of the movement in 1988 must be interpreted as a reaction to and at least a partial rejection of the economic liberalism and the severe costs it meted out.

The 1980s in Mexico was thus a period of multifaceted change which saw a dramatic shift of economic policy, rising opposition to the state-labor alliance, and a widespread sense that the one-party-dominant regime should be abandoned, accompanied by broad support for a more competitive regime. The economic change was the clearest, representing a virtual about-face in policy. But the extent of political change remained uncertain.

In assessing the political changes that are currently occurring in Mexico, we may return to the issues of the party system and the social base of the state. Three possibilities were suggested in Chapter 4. One type of change consists of slight alterations in the party system in the direction of more accommodation to opposition parties and greater competitiveness. Changes of this type might nonetheless leave intact the support base of the state and the overall coalitional pattern, as well as the dominant position of the PRI. A second possibility is a more significant change in the party's coalition and in the social base of the state, most important a change that would disarticulate the coalition with labor. This may be accompanied by either a similar kind of continuity or reproduction of the party system, or some real but limited liberalizing changes, such as a change in the PRI's status from a dominant to a majority or plurality party. Such changes could be compatible with quite a different distribution of power stemming from significantly more opposition victories, though at the least the PRI would be first among equals.

The third possibility is more thoroughgoing change of both the coalitional basis of the state and the party system, involving a liberalizing move to a fully competitive, multi-party regime. The goal of the opposition on both the left and the right has been to achieve this third type of more fundamental change. The future of the Cardenists is dependent on the move to a more competitive electoral regime. In addition, they would prefer a regime more firmly rooted in the popular classes, and they see the state-labor alliance as an obstacle, a cooptive instrument which deprives labor of its autonomy and deprives the Cardenists of a potential source of electoral support. As an opposition party, the PAN has a similar interest in a more open regime, and it too supports the disarticulation of the state-labor alliance but for quite a different reason—as a way to prevent what it sees as the episodic "populist" indiscretions committed by the PRI in the past.

With regard to the goal of the PRI government, many analysts have interpreted its current strategy as promoting the first type of change—slight alterations that seek above all to preserve the existing regime. Such changes indeed took place through the 1960s and 1970s. By contrast, the present study has interpreted government policy since 1985 as pursuing a strategy along the lines of the second alternative. This interpretation points to two new features of Mexican politics. First, the Mexican government has changed its position with respect to the desirability of the state-labor alliance. Key state actors, particularly within the presidency, no longer support the alliance or find it useful—at least in its traditional form. The second new feature is that in the 1980s, the Mexican government came to favor the liberalization of the one-party-dominant regime. That regime, with its primary appeal to revolutionary rather than democratic legitimacy, no longer serves the government well. Rather, the government sees in political liberalization not only a solution to the earlier problems of legitimacy, but also the basis for a new regime that will be more consistent with the commitment to more market-oriented economic policies. Hence, the government now seems ready to support a move to a more competitive political regime—but with the proviso that the party challenge that may emerge will not soon displace the PRI from at least a plurality position, nor offer a real economic alternative to the new market orientation. Rather it must contribute to a broad consensus on economic as well as political goals.

It might be noted that this instrumental, and hence ambivalent, position of the government toward political opening is consistent with other historical processes of democratization. Recent literature on the current wave of democratization has tended to downplay the degree to which democracy is pursued to achieve economic policy goals. In the 1990s, no one can deny that democracy has come to be widely valued as an end in itself. With this recognition, however, we should not forget that political actors may also favor a democratic regime as a means to other, nonpolitical ends. Democratization does not serve only to legitimate rule, to address incumbency and succession issues, and to resolve conflict. In addition, democracy is promoted to advance a substantive policy agenda and defend material interests. Democratization is not simply the process of negotiation and bargaining whereby groups agree to abide by a structure of institutionalized uncertainty. It is a process whereby groups write rules that shape and limit the scope of that uncertainty, often to favor a particular substantive project. In this regard, the electoral laws sponsored by the Mexican government are not an aberration in the process of political liberalization: the making or reforming of democratic constitutions is often a process through which varied substantive goals are pursued in negotiations over electoral procedures. It is in this way that one should understand the strategy of the Mexican government—its declared commitment to democratization, as well as its electoral engineering and even its retreat to fraud and coercive manipulation that seem to belie that commitment. What is involved is the oxymoronic attempt to use manipulation in constructing a "safe" competitive regime.

Though for quite different—even contradictory—reasons both the Mexican government and the opposition now seem to favor political liberalization, the nature of political change in Mexico remains unclear. Of the major parties, the PRD has had the strongest commitment to political liberalization. The PAN has been more willing to compromise with the government out of fear that the PRD would be the greatest beneficiary of more open competitive politics. The PRI government remains even more uncertain, since it wants to protect both its new economic policy and its ability to govern the country. It seems ready to disarticulate the coalition with labor for economic reasons, but fears it may have to rely on labor support in a more competitive regime. Hence it seeks liberalization, but under the condition that it can structure the outcome to prevent the emergence of a significant challenge on the left that would be capable of moving into the political vacuum created by the PRI government's growing abandonment of its alliance with the labor movement.

Given these ambivalences, the direction of regime evolution remains unclear. At the very least, it would seem that the one-party-dominant regime will undergo some liberalization, though these changes may remain limited; at the most, the one-party-dominant regime may be superseded. The scope of political liberalization will depend on two things. The first is the success of the government in structuring the political opposition so that competition will not endanger its economic policy—either because the opposition remains too weak (or is sufficiently weakened) or because a significant opposition challenge will arise (or be tolerated) only from a party which shares the government's economic agenda—that is, from the PAN and not the PRD. The second is the success of the government in maintaining control of the liberalizing project, or conversely the success of the opposition in undercutting the government's control. To some degree, then, the Mexican regime seems to be embarked on a course of liberalization, be it more limited or more extensive. Either way, however, the coalitional basis of the state seems to be undergoing a profound change. In this sense, at least, the one-party-dominant regime with its base in the state-labor alliance, the regime that has characterized Mexico through most of the twentieth century, is unlikely to survive in its earlier form.

ADDENDUM: THE 1991 MIDTERM ELECTIONS

On 18 August 1991, midterm elections were held for half of the Mexican senators, all federal deputies, and six governors. These elections seemed to underscore a number of points made in the analysis above.

The official results registered a landslide victory for the PRI. In pre-electoral opinion polls and in the official returns, the PRI showed a remarkable recovery; indeed the PRI vote nationwide rose to over 60 percent, not quite recapturing its traditional level of three-fourths of the electorate, but nevertheless returning to a position of overwhelming dominance. In the vote for the Chamber of Deputies, the PAN won 17.7 percent, retaining the level of electoral support of the prior decade or so, while the FDN parties together won about the same (16.7 percent). Of course, the FDN coalition had fallen apart, so that the PRD came in third at 8.3 percent, and the satellite parties, which had captured most of the FDN vote in 1988, together totaled about the same as the PRD (8.4 percent).

This vote translated into the following victories. The PRI won all but one of the senate seats (the PAN won a seat in Baja California Norte) and all of the governorships, though two of these elections were marred by fraud and new elections were called (see below). In the Chamber of Deputies the PRI won 290 of the 300 seats in the single-member constituencies, with the rest going to the PAN. Once the proportional representation seats were allocated, the total distribution of seats was 64 percent for the PRI, 17.8 percent for the PAN, 8.2 percent for the PRD, 4.6 percent for the PFCRN, 3 percent for the PARM, and 2.4 percent for the PPS (*Latin America Weekly Report*, 15 August and 5 September 1991).

How are these results to be interpreted? In many ways, this election looked like a restoration of the familiar Mexican system. It was certainly clear that in the brief span from the 1988 elections to those in 1991—a span that saw the demise of one-party rule in Eastern Europe and the Soviet Union (the Mexican elections actually took place on the day of the failed Soviet coup)—the Mexican dominant-party system had taken a very different path. Two inter-related questions arise. How does one account for the PRI landslide? Did it indicate a resurgence of the old regime, representing a dominant PRI based on the old coalition, or a step toward a "reformed" (re-formed) regime along the lines described above as the vision of the modernizers?

Several explanations have been given for the PRI landslide. One is the weakness of the opposition, a weakness, as noted, that was certainly promoted by the obstacles thrown up by the government. The PAN has never convincingly demonstrated an ability to move much beyond its traditional locus and level of support. Similarly, it was apparent from the outset that the PRD was having trouble extending its organization as an effective political party. The 1991 elections highlighted just how great those difficulties have been. The PRD's problems were compounded by the necessity of fighting these elections as a new party without the advantage of Cárdenas at the head of the ticket. The test of the party's potential for becoming a more central political player will come in 1994, with the next presidential elections.

A second explanation has to do with the achievements of the PRI. The party functioned as a well-oiled machine and undertook a big effort to mobilize the vote. The tactics included the usual array of tricks in the ward-healing repertoire, including block-level organization, free breakfasts, and transportation to the polls. Taking a somewhat longer view of voter mobilization, PRI activists point to the reform and revitalization of the party and the way it succeeded in recruiting more popular representatives to stand as candidates. There are no studies or evidence to evaluate the degree to which a rejuvenation of this kind may indeed have occurred, though many analysts have noted some improvement in the quality of the party's candidates. More easily substantiated is the success of certain policies undertaken by the Salinas government. After the "lost decade"—the de la Madrid sexenio, which saw economic stagnation, Mexico's first experience with triple-digit inflation, and dramatically plunging living standards—Salinas managed to engineer a modest but nevertheless welcome renewal of economic growth and to bring inflation under control.

Also winning support for the PRI was the new National Solidarity Program (Pronasol). In many ways, this was one of those double-edged programs which have been characteristic of Mexican politics. On the one hand, as the government has presented it, it is an anti-poverty, community development program built around public works projects based on self-help. It resonates with development orientations toward empowerment and decentralization, and it has been suggested that it was based on Salinas's thesis at Harvard University (*New York Times*, 16 August 1991).

On the other hand, this program has been seen by critics as small compensation for the government's poverty-creating economic policies and the toll they have exacted in terms of declining wages and unemployment. More to the present point, Pronasol, instituted in the first year of the Salinas government shortly after the PRI's 1988 electoral setback, has served several political purposes of the government and the PRI. It was a useful tool for the PRI machine in making available the nearly $4 billion appropriated from state revenues for pork-barrel projects (*New York Times*, 16 August 1991). In dispersing funds, the government targeted areas of opposition strength where it wanted to win back political support; in short, Pronasol was used as part of the government's partisan electoral strategy. In addition, the program was used in an attempt to advance the PRI's renewal and enhance its grass-roots popularity: the projects have, at least potentially, been a mechanism for identifying community leaders who can be groomed as PRI candidates for local office (*New York Times*, 16 September 1991).

A third reason given for the PRI landslide is electoral fraud. That fraud occurred is indisputable, though virtually all accounts suggest that the PRI would have won either comfortably or perhaps even overwhelmingly without it. What remains open to speculation is the degree to which fraud occurred and who the main perpetrators were.

One interpretation is that Salinas had every reason to want a clean election. He had promised one, he had not needed fraud for a PRI victory, and a clean election was necessary to demonstrate that Mexico was a politically worthy partner and collaborator in an emerging democratic North American community. In this interpretation, the fraud was relatively limited and localized, concentrated primarily in three states. Furthermore, the fraud was the work of local political bosses whom the center was unable or ultimately unwilling to control.

$\cancel{B})$ According to another interpretation, fraud was widespread and directed from the presidency itself. It represented a calculated gamble by Salinas, acting on another goal: to turn the election into a referendum on his economic policies and to demonstrate to the United States an overwhelming mandate for entering into a North American Free Trade Agreement. According to this interpretation, the fraud was pervasive and necessary to demonstrate such a clear, overwhelming mandate, something that would have eluded Salinas if he had settled merely for a clean plurality.*

Where does this leave us with respect to the question about the retreat from or advance of the modernizers' reform program? It was suggested above that the unexpected electoral challenge in 1988 introduced a number of reasons for ambivalence concerning continued commitment to that project. In which direction do the 1991 elections point?

The style of macroeconomic policy-making, distributive pork-barrel programs, and fraud all conjure up images of a return to (or continuation of) business as usual. The relatively successful attack on inflation was accomplished through reliance on the government-engineered social pact between business and labor groups, thus revealing a certain ongoing dependence of the government on labor cooperation for achieving policy goals. Pronasol looks like a continuation of old-style, clientelistic distributive machine politics, not a new-style, technocratic pattern of policy-making. Furthermore, given the partisan use that the government has made of the program, it is seen as perpetuating the official-party or state-party status of the PRI and hence undermining any potential move toward free competition among parties on an equal footing. The electoral fraud has seemed like a definitive inability or unwillingness of the government to move forward with its proclaimed political modernization program, given its advertised commitment to clean elections.

If the government is bent on an overwhelming PRI victory and a perpetuation of results that preserve the "clean sweep" of virtually all elected posts for the PRI; if it continues to resort to electoral fraud; if it remains dependent on "populist" economic policies, machine

*This interpretation was advanced by Jorge Castañeda in a lecture at the University of California, Berkeley, 11 October 1991. Castañeda suggests that grossly inflated, fraudulent figures for the PRI in the official returns account for the substantial increase in the total 1991 vote over 1988.

politics, and official-party status; and if it continues to rely on the cooperation of organized labor for its macroeconomic policies, then it appears that the Salinas modernizers have not stayed on track.

Before we rest with this conclusion, however, some other considerations must be borne in mind. The continuation of the social pact and Pronasol notwithstanding, the government did not significantly stray from its neo-liberal economic path in the face of these elections, nor indeed did it make the concessions to labor that used to be part of the state-labor coalition. It is an eloquent if discouraging comment on the increasing weakness of labor that the government did not significantly compromise its economic program even as it managed to renew the social pact.

If the economic policy has remained on track, what about the political modernization project? The modernizers' project as laid out above was limited. It was seen as an instrumental project to address the question of legitimacy and to create a new dominant coalition more consistent with economic liberalization. It was a project to decorporatize the party and to institute a more competitive regime, primarily to disarticulate the alliance with labor; it was not a project to oust the PRI from power or to deprive it of certain advantages of incumbency.

This project has not necessarily been derailed. Pronasol should be seen not only as a perpetuation of traditional electoral politics, but at least equally as part of the government's effort to alter the constituency of the PRI. It has been a vehicle for circumventing the traditional sectors of the PRI—most importantly organized labor—and establishing links to other mass constituencies. The program has been aimed at gaining popular support among the urban poor and their community organizations in lower class *barrios*, a sector that has not historically been embraced by the party. The PRI finds it advantageous to appeal to this sector, both because it is the locus of new and potentially important opposition movements against the government and because its demands do not, to the same extent, undermine liberal market policies.

Nor is the election itself evidence that the government's modernization program was stillborn, despite the fraud. The disposition of the most flagrant cases of fraud may be telling. These cases concerned two gubernatorial contests where tough electoral battles had been anticipated: in San Luis Potosí, where the PRD and PAN backed a unified opposition candidate, and in Guanajuato, where a popular Coca Cola executive ran as the PAN candidate. After sustained protests and widespread complaints of fraud, the declared PRI winners resigned, and interim governors took office until new elections could be called. Virtually all accounts suggested that Salinas himself was behind the cancellation of these PRI victories, acting out of sensitivity to international criticism as revealed in the international press, including a stinging editorial in the *New York Times*. In other words, the Salinas intervention occurred to advance the economic project, for which it was necessary not only to adjust the internal coalition, but also to make Mexico appear a credible and politically worthy partner and collaborator, a participant in an emerging democratic North American community.

A + B not sufficient

Neither of the two interpretations of the fraud presented above constitutes a convincing or sufficient argument that the political project of the modernizers has been rejected. If fraud was limited and locally perpetrated against the preferences of the president, then, given the instrumental nature of the reforms and their functionality for the economic program, there is room to expect further pressure from the center for political reform of both the party and the electoral process—since the new law has made democracy safe for the PRI. If the fraud was a calculated gamble directed by Salinas himself to demonstrate a mandate for the FTA, then we can expect that motive to weaken once the agreement becomes a fait accompli, at which time the international pressure for democracy will outweigh the pressure for a mandate. According to both of these interpretations, the PRI should be willing to settle into a more competitive system in which it can live comfortably with a much reduced vote, perhaps even a mere plurality. The coalitional logic of its liberal economic policy points to this, and the logic of the new electoral law seems to provide for it.

Therefore, the political liberalization "project from above"— that is, the state project or the modernizers' project—seems in place. The big variable remains how the opposition project will shape up to challenge and push it farther in the direction of a more open regime to the point where political competition will produce the alternation of parties in power and meaningful debate and choices on public issues.

BIBLIOGRAPHY

Aguilar García, Javier. 1985. "Los sindicatos nacionales." In *Organización y sindicalismo*, ed. Pablo Gonzalez Casanova, Samuel Leon, and Ignacio Marván. Vol. 3 of *El obrero mexicano*. Mexico City: Siglo Veintiuno.

Alexander, Robert J. 1957. *Communism in Latin America*. New Brunswick, N.J.: Rutgers University Press.

Alvarado Mendoza, Arturo. 1987. "Introduction." In *Electoral Patterns and Perspectives in Mexico*, ed. Arturo Alvarado Mendoza. San Diego: Center for U.S.-Mexican Studies, University of California.

Anderson, Bo, and Cockcroft, James D. 1972. "Control and Co-optation in Mexican Politics." In Cockcroft et al., eds.

Anguiano, Arturo. 1975. *El estado y la política obrera del cardenismo*. Mexico City: Ediciones Era.

————. 1988. "Toward a Unified Left Perspective." *Against the Current* 3, 5 (November–December, new series): 33–36.

Ashby, Joe C. 1967. *Organized Labor and the Mexican Revolution under Lázaro Cárdenas*. Chapel Hill: University of North Carolina Press.

Ayala, José; Blanco, José; Cordera, Rolando; Knockenbauer, Guillermo; and Labra, Armando. 1980. "La crisis económica: Evolución y perspectivas." In Gonzales Casanova and Florescano, eds.

Baer, Delal, and Bailey, John. 1985. "Mexico's 1985 Midterm Elections: A Preliminary Assessment." *LASA Forum* 16, 3 (Fall).

Bailey, John J. 1985. "Mexico." In Hopkins, ed., vol. 3 (1983–84).

————. 1987. "Can the PRI Be Reformed? Decentralizing Candidate Selection." In Gentleman, ed.

————. 1988. *Governing Mexico*. New York: St. Martin's Press.

Basurto, Jorge. 1983. *En el régimen de Luis Echeverría*. Vol. 14 of *La clase obrera en la historia de México*. Mexico City: Siglo Veintiuno.

————. 1984. *Del avilacamachismo al alemanismo (1940–1952)*. Vol. 11 of *La clase obrera en la historia de México*. Mexico City: Siglo Veintiuno.

Brandenburg, Frank. 1964. *The Making of Modern Mexico*. Englewood Cliffs, N.J.: Prentice-Hall.

Camacho, Manuel. 1976. "Control sobre el movimiento obrero en México." *Foro Internacional* 16, 4 (April–June): 496–525.

————. 1980. *El futuro inmediato.* Vol. 15 of *La clase obrera en la historia de México.* Mexico City: Siglo Veintiuno.

Camp, Roderic A. 1984. "Mexico." In Hopkins, ed., vol. 2 (1982–83).

————. 1986. "Mexico." In Hopkins, ed., vol. 4 (1984–85).

Camp, Roderic A., ed. 1986. *Mexico's Political Stability: The Next Five Years.* Boulder: Westview Press.

Campbell, Bruce. 1991. "Beggar Thy Neighbor." *Report on the Americas* 24, 6 (May): 22–29.

Carr, Barry. 1972. "Organized Labour and the Mexican Revolution, 1915–1928." Latin American Centre, St. Antony's College, Oxford University. Occasional Papers II.

————. 1976. *El movimiento obrero y la política en México, 1910–1929.* Mexico City: Secretaría de Educación Pública.

————. 1981. "The Development of Communism and Marxism in Mexico: A Historiographical Essay." Paper presented at the Sixth Conference of Mexican and United States Historians, Chicago.

————. 1983. "The Mexican Economic Debacle and the Labor Movement: A New Era or More of the Same?" In *Mexico's Economic Crisis: Challenges and Opportunities,* ed. Donald L. Wyman. San Diego: Center for U.S.-Mexican Studies, University of California. Monograph Series No. 12.

————. 1985. *Mexican Communism, 1968-1983: Eurocommunism in the Americas?* San Diego: Center for U.S.-Mexican Studies, University of California. Research Report Series No. 42.

Carr, Barry, and Anzaldua Montoya, Ricardo, eds. 1986. *The Mexican Left: Popular Movements and the Politics of Austerity.* San Diego: Center for U.S.-Mexican Studies, University of California. Monograph Series, No. 18.

Carreño Carlón, José. 1988. "The Transfer of Power in Mexico." Presented at the conference on Presidential Succession: Bi-National Reflections, 7 October, University of California, Los Angeles.

Castañeda, Jorge. 1989a. "Mexico." In *Latin America and Caribbean Contemporary Record,* vol. 6 (1986–87), ed. Abraham F. Lowenthal. New York: Holmes and Meier.

————. 1989b. In *Los Angeles Times,* 1 January.

Clark, Marjorie Ruth. 1973. *Organized Labor in Mexico.* Chapel Hill: University of North Carolina Press.

Cleaves, Peter S. 1987. *Professions and the State: The Mexican Case.* Tucson: University of Arizona Press.

Cockcroft, James D., et al., eds. 1972. *Dependence and Underdevelopment: Latin America's Political Economy.* Garden City, N.Y.: Anchor Books.

Collier, Ruth Berins, and Collier, David. 1991. *Shaping the Political Arena: Critical Junctures, the Labor Movement, and Regime Dynamics in Latin America.* Princeton: Princeton University Press.

————. 1979. "Inducements versus Constraints: Disaggregating Corporatism." *American Political Science Review* 73, 4 (December): 967–86.

Cook, Maria Lorena. 1990. "Organizing Opposition in the Teachers' Movement in Oaxaca." In *Popular Movements and Political Change in Mexico*, ed. Joe Foweraker and Ann L. Craig. Boulder: Lynne Rienner.

Córdova, Arnaldo. 1972. *La formación del poder político en México*. Mexico City: Ediciones Era.

————. 1973. *La ideología de la Revolución Mexicana: La formación del nuevo régimen*. Mexico City: Ediciones Era.

————. 1974. *La política de masas del cardenismo*. Mexico City: Ediciones Era.

————. 1976. "La transformación del PNR en PRM: El triunfo del corporativismo en México." In *Contemporary Mexico: Papers of the Fourth International Congress of Mexican History*, ed. James W. Wilkie, Michael C. Meyer, and Edna Monzón de Wilkie. Los Angeles: Latin American Center, UCLA. Latin American Studies Series, vol. 29.

————. 1981. *En una época de crisis (1928–1934)*. Vol. 9 of *La clase obrera en la historia de México*, ed. Pablo González Casanova. Mexico City: Siglo Veintiuno.

Cornelius, Wayne A. 1973. "Nation Building, Participation, and Distribution: The Politics of Social Reform under Cardenas." In *Crisis, Choice, and Change: Historical Studies of Political Development*, ed. Gabriel Almond et al. Boston: Little, Brown.

————. 1986. "Political Liberalization and the 1985 Elections in Mexico." In *Elections and Democratization in Latin America, 1980–85*, ed. Paul W. Drake and Eduardo Silva. San Diego: Center for Iberian and Latin American Studies, University of California.

————. 1987. "Mexico." In *Latin America and Caribbean Contemporary Record*, vol. 5 (1985–86), ed. Abraham F. Lowenthal. New York: Holmes and Meier.

Cornelius, Wayne A.; Gentleman, Judith; and Smith, Peter H. 1989. "Overview: The Dynamics of Political Change in Mexico." In Cornelius, Gentleman, and Smith, eds.

Cornelius, Wayne A.; Gentleman, Judith; and Smith, Peter H., eds. 1989. *Mexico's Alternative Political Futures*. San Diego: Center for U.S.-Mexican Studies, University of California.

Dulles, John W. F. 1961. *Yesterday in Mexico: A Chronicle of the Revolution, 1919–1936*. Austin: University of Texas Press.

Easton, David. 1965. *A Systems Analysis of Political Life*. New York: John Wiley and Sons.

Escobar, Saúl. 1988. "Elections Without Legitimacy." *The Other Side of Mexico* 6 (July–September): 1–5.

Everett, Michael D. 1967. "The Role of the Mexican Trade Unions, 1950–1963." Doctoral dissertation, Department of Economics, Washington University.

Foro Nacional de Consulta sobre las Relaciones Comerciales de México con el Mundo. 1990. "Foro sobre la política comercial de México: Informe final" (Comisión organizada del Senado). *Comercio Exterior* 40, 6 (June).

Frieden, Jeffry. 1989. "Winners and Losers in the Latin American Debt Crisis: The Political Implications." In Stallings and Kaufman, eds.

Fuentes Díaz, Vicente. 1959. "Desarrollo y evolución del movimiento obrero a partir de 1929." *Revista de Ciencias Políticas y Sociales* 5, 17 (July–September): 325–48.

Furtak, Robert K. 1974. *El partido de la revolución y la estabilidad política en México.* Mexico: UNAM, Serie Estudios 35.

Garrido, Luis Javier. 1984. *El partido de la revolución institucionalizada: La formación del nuevo estado en México, 1928–1945.* México City: Siglo Veintiuno.

Garza, David T. 1964. "Factionalism in the Mexican Left: The Frustration of the MLN." *Western Political Quarterly* 17, 3 (September): 447–60.

Gentleman, Judith, ed. 1987. *Mexican Politics in Transition.* Boulder: Westview Press.

Gómez, Leopoldo, and Klesner, Joseph L. 1988. "Mexico's 1988 Elections: The Beginning of a New Era of Mexican Politics?" *LASA Forum* 19, 3 (Fall): 1–8.

González Casanova, Pablo. 1982. *El estado y los partidos políticos en México.* Mexico City: Ediciones Era.

González Casanova, Pablo, and Florescano, Enrique, eds. 1980. *México, hoy.* Mexico City: Siglo Veintiuno.

Grayson, George. 1988. *Oil and Mexican Foreign Policy.* Pittsburgh: University of Pittsburgh Press.

Gutiérrez Garza, Esthela. 1988. "De la relación salarial monopolista a la flexibilidad del trabajo, México 1960–1986." In *La crisis del estado del bienestar,* ed. E. Gutiérrez Garza. Vol. 2 of *Testimonios de la crisis.* Mexico City: Siglo Veintiuno.

Hamilton, Nora. 1982. *The Limits of State Autonomy.* Princeton: Princeton University Press.

Handelman, Howard. 1976. "The Politics of Labor Protest in Mexico." *Journal of Inter-American Studies and World Affairs* 18, 3 (August): 267–94.

————. 1979. "Organized Labor in Mexico: Oligarchy and Dissent." American Universities Field Staff Reports, North America Series, No. 18.

Harker, Mary Margaret. 1937. "The Organization of Labor in Mexico since 1910." Doctoral dissertation, Department of History, University of Southern California.

Hayes, James Riley. 1951. "The Mexican Labor Movement, 1931–1951." M.A. thesis, University of California, Berkeley.

Hernández Cháves, Alicia. 1979. *La mecánica cardenista, 1934-1940.* Vol. 16 of *Historia de la Revolución Méxicana.* México City: El Colegio de México.

Hopkins, Jack, ed. 1982–85. *Latin America and Caribbean Contemporary Record,* vols. 2 (1982–83), 3 (1983–84), and 4 (1984–85). New York: Holmes and Meier.

Johnson, Kenneth F. 1971. *Mexican Democracy: A Critical Review.* Boston: Allyn and Bacon.

————. 1978. *Mexican Democracy: A Critical Review,* rev. ed. New York: Praeger.

Kaufman, Robert R. 1988. *The Politics of Debt in Argentina, Brazil, and Mexico: Economic Stabilization in the 1980s.* Berkeley: Institute of International Studies.

Lasswell, Harold D., and Kaplan, Abraham. 1950. *Power and Society: A Framework for Political Inquiry.* New Haven: Yale University Press.

Leal, Juan Felipe. 1976. *México: Estado, burocracia, y sindicatos.* Mexico City: Ediciones El Caballito.

————. 1985. "Las estructuras sindicales." In *Organización y sindicalismo.* Vol. 3 of *El obrero mexicano,* ed. Pablo González Casanova, Samuel León, and Ignacio Marván. Mexico City: Siglo Veintiuno.

León, Samuel, and Marván, Ignacio. 1985. *En el cardenismo (1934–1940).* Vol. 10 of *La clase obrera en la historia de México.* Mexico City: Siglo Veintiuno.

León, Samuel, and Xelhuantzi López, Maria. 1985. "Los obreros, las burocracias sindicales y la politica del gobierno." In *La política y la cultura.* Vol. 5 of *El obrero mexicano,* ed. Pablo González Casanova, Samuel León, and Ignacio Marván. Mexico City: Siglo Veintiuno.

Levy, Daniel C., and Székely, Gabriel. 1983. *Mexico: Paradoxes of Stability and Change.* Boulder: Westview Press.

Loaeza, Soledad. 1987. "El Partido Acción Nacional: De la oposición leal a la impaciencia electoral." In *La vida política mexicana en la crisis,* ed. Soledad Loaeza and Rafael Segovia. Mexico City: El Colegio de México.

Locke, Richard M. 1990. "In Search of Flexibility: Industrial Restructuring and Industrial Relations in the Italian Automobile Industry." Mimeo.

López Aparicio, Alfonso. 1952. *El movimiento obrero en México: antecedentes, desarrollo y tendencias.* Mexico City: Editorial Jus.

Loyo Brambila, Aurora, and Pozas Horcasitas, Ricardo. 1975. "Notes on the Mechanisms of Control Exercised by the Mexican State over the Organized Sector of the Working Class. A Case Study: The Political Crisis of 1958." National University of Mexico, Institute of Social Research, April.

Luna, Matilde; Tirado, Ricardo; and Valdes, Francisco. 1987. "Businessmen and Politics in Mexico, 1982–1986." In *Government and Private Sector in Contemporary Mexico,* ed. Sylvia Maxfield and Ricardo Anzaldua Montoya. San Diego: Center for U.S.-Mexican Studies, University of California.

Madrazo Pintado, Roberto. 1989. "The Political Modernization of the Institutional Revolutionary Party." Paper presented 17 October, University of California, Berkeley. Mexico: Secretaría de Organización del CEN, PRI.

Marván, Ignacio. 1985. "El proyecto nacional de las organizaciones obreras." In *La pólitica y la cultura*. Vol. 5. Mexico City: Siglo Veintiuno.

Maxfield, Sylvia. 1989. "National Business, Debt-Led Growth, and Political Transition in Latin America." In Stallings and Kaufman, eds.

Medín, Tzvi. 1982. *El Minimato presidencial: Historia política del Maximato (1928–1935)*. Mexico City: Ediciones Era.

Medina, Luis. 1978. *Del cardenismo al avilacamachismo*. Vol. 18 of *Historia de la Revolución Méxicana*. Mexico City: El Colegio de México.

————. 1979. *Civilismo y modernización del autoritarianismo, 1949–1952*. Vol. 20 of *Historia de la Revolución Méxicana*. Mexico City: El Colegio de México.

Meyer, Jean, et al. 1977. *Estado y sociedad con Calles, 1924–1928*. Vol. 11 of *Historia de la Revolución Méxicana*. Mexico City: El Colegio de México.

Meyer, Lorenzo. 1976. "La Encrucijada." In *Historia general de México*, vol. 2, ed. Daniel Cosío Villegas. Mexico City: El Colegio de México.

————. 1978. *El conflicto social de los gobiernos del Maximato, 1928–1934*. Vol. 13 of *Historia de la Revolución Méxicana*. Mexico City: El Colegio de México.

————. 1989. "Democratization of the PRI: Mission Impossible?" In Cornelius, Gentleman, and Smith, eds.

Meyer, Lorenzo, et al. 1978. *Los inicios de la institucionalización, 1928–1934*. Vol. 12 of *Historia de la Revolución Méxicana*. México City: El Colegio de México.

Michaels, Albert L. 1966. "Mexican Politics and Nationalism from Calles to Cárdenas." Doctoral dissertation, Department of History, University of Pennsylvania.

Middlebrook, Kevin J. 1981. "Political Change and Political Reform in an Authoritarian Regime: The Case of Mexico." Washington, D.C.: Latin America Program of the Woodrow Wilson International Center for Scholars, Smithsonian Institution. Working Paper No. 103.

————. 1988. "Dilemmas of Change in Mexican Politics." *World Politics* 41 (October): 120–41.

————. 1989. "The Sounds of Silence: Organised Labour's Response to Economic Crisis in Mexico." *Journal of Latin American Studies* 21, 2 (May): 195–220.

Miller, Richard U. 1966. "The Role of Labor Organizations in a Developing Country: The Case of Mexico." Doctoral dissertation, New York State University, School of Industrial and Labor Relations.

Molinar Horcasitas, Juan. 1987. "The 1985 Federal Elections in Mexico: The Product of a System." In *Electoral Patterns and Perspectives in Mexico*, ed. Arturo Alvarado Mendoza. San Diego: Center for U.S.-Mexican Studies, University of California. Monograph Series, No. 22.

————. 1989. "The Future of the Electoral System." In Cornelius, Gentleman, and Smith, eds.

Munck, Gerardo. 1990. "State Power and Labor Politics in the Context of Military Rule: Organized Labor, Peronism, and the Armed Forces in Argentina, 1976–1983." Doctoral dissertation, Department of Political Science, University of California, San Diego.

Needler, Martin. 1987. "The Significance of Recent Events for the Mexican Political System." In Gentleman, ed.

Newell, Roberto, and Rubio F., Luis. 1984. *Mexico's Dilemma: The Political Origins of Economic Crisis*. Boulder: Westview Press.

North, Liisa, and Raby, David. 1977. "The Dynamic of Revolution and Counterrevolution: Mexico under Cárdenas, 1934–1940." *Latin American Research Unit Studies* 2, 1 (October): 23–56.

Nuncio, Abraham. 1986. *El PAN: Alternativa de poder o instrumento de la oligarquía empresarial*. Mexico City: Nueva Imagen.

O'Donnell, Guillermo, and Schmitter, Philippe C. 1986. *Transitions from Authoritarian Rule: Tentative Conclusions about Uncertain Democracies*. Baltimore: Johns Hopkins University Press.

Pellicer de Brody, Olga, and Reyna, José Luis. 1978. *El afranzamiento de la estabilidad política, 1952–1960. Historia de la Revolución Mexicana*. Mexico City: El Colegio de México.

Portes, Alejandro. 1977. "Legislatures under Authoritarian Regimes: The Case of Mexico." *Journal of Political and Military Sociology* 5, 2 (Fall): 185–201.

PRI. 1989. *Comparativos de los resultados electorales 1988–1989*. Mexico City: Secretaría de Organización del CEN, PRI.

Prieto, Ana Maria. 1986. "Mexico's National Coordinadores in a Context of Economic Crisis." In Carr and Anzaldua Montoya, eds.

Purcell, Susan Kaufman. 1978. "Clientelism and Development in Mexico." Paper presented at a conference on Political Clientelism, Patronage and Development, Italy.

Reding, Andrew. 1988. "Mexico at a Crossroads: The 1988 Election and Beyond." *World Policy Journal* 5, 4: 615–49.

Reyna, José Luis, and Miquet, Marcelo. 1976. "Introducción a la historia de las organizaciones obreras en México: 1912–1966." In *Tres estudios sobre el movimiento obrero en México*, ed. José Luis Reyna et al. Mexico City: El Colegio de México.

Reyna, José Luis, and Trejo Delarbre, Raúl. 1981. *De Adolfo Ruiz Cortines a Adolfo López Mateos, 1952–1964*. Vol. 12 of *La clase obrera en la historia de México*. Mexico City: Siglo Veintiuno.

Rivera Castro, José. 1983. *En la presidencia de Plutarco Elías Calles, 1924–1928*. Vol. 8 of *La clase obrera en México*. Mexico City: Siglo Veintiuno.

Rodriguez, Victoria Elizabeth. 1987. "The Politics of Decentralization in Mexico: Divergent Outcomes of Policy Implementation." Doctoral dissertation, Department of Political Science, University of California, Berkeley.

Rodríguez Araujo, Octavi. 1982. *La reforma política y los partidos en México.* Mexico City: Siglo Veintiuno.

Roxborough, Ian. 1989. "Organized Labor: A Major Victim of the Debt Crisis." In Stallings and Kaufman, eds.

Salazar-Carrillo, Jorge. 1982. *The Structure of Wages in Latin American Manufacturing Industries.* Miami: University Presses of Florida.

Salinas de Gortari, Carlos. 1990. "Foro sobre la política comercial de México: Cinco premisas sobre las relaciones comerciales con el exterior." *Comercio Exterior* 40, 6 (June).

Saragoza, Alex. 1988. *The Monterrey Elite and the Mexican State, 1880–1940.* Austin: University of Texas Press.

Schneider, Ben. 1988–89. "Partly for Sale: Privatization and State Strength in Brazil and Mexico." *Journal of Inter-American Studies and World Affairs* 30, 4 (Winter).

Scott, Robert E. 1964. *Mexican Government in Transition.* Urbana: University of Illinois Press.

Semo, Enrique. 1986. "The Mexican Left and the Economic Crisis." In Carr and Anzaldua Montoya, eds.

Semo, Ilán. 1982. "El ocaso de los mitos (1958–1968)." In *Mexico: Un pueblo en la historia,* vol. 4, ed. Enrique Semo. Mexico City: Nueva Imagen.

Smith, Peter H. 1978. "The Breakdown of Democracy in Argentina, 1916-1930." In *The Breakdown of Democratic Regimes: Latin America,* ed. Juan J. Linz and Alfred Stepan. Baltimore: Johns Hopkins University Press.

—————. 1986. "Leadership and Change: Intellectuals and Technocrats in Mexico." In Camp, ed.

Stallings, Barbara, and Kaufman, Robert, eds. 1989. *Debt and Democracy in Latin America.* Boulder: Westview Press.

Stevens, Evelyn P. 1974. *Protest and Response in Mexico.* Cambridge, Mass.: MIT Press.

—————. 1987. "The Opposition in Mexico: Always a Bridesmaid, Never Yet the Bride." In Gentleman, ed.

Story, Dale. 1983. "Industrial Elites in Mexico: Political Ideology and Influence." *Journal of Interamerican Studies and World Affairs* 25, 3 (August): 351–76.

—————. 1987. "The PAN, the Private Sector and the Future of the Mexican Opposition." In Gentleman, ed.

Taylor, Philip B., Jr. 1960. *Government and Politics of Uruguay.* New Orleans: Tulane University Press.

Thompson, John K. 1979. *Inflation, Financial Markets, and Economic Development: The Experience of Mexico.* Greenwich: JAI Press.

Trejo Delarbre, Raúl. 1980. "El movimiento obrero: Situación y perspectivas." In González Casanova and Florescano, eds.

————. 1985. "Sindicatos y proyecto nacional en la crisis de hoy." In *México: Presente y futuro*, ed. Jorge Alcocer. Mexico City: Ediciones de Cultura Popular.

————. 1987. "La paralisis obrera." *Nexos*, April, pp. 37–64.

United Nations. 1989. *Economic Survey of Latin America and the Caribbean, 1988.* Santiago.

United States, Department of Labor, Bureau of Labor Statistics, Office of Productivity and Technology. 1990. "Hourly Compensation Costs for Production Workers in Manufacturing, 34 Countries." Unpublished data. April.

Vásquez Rubio, Pilar. 1988. "The End of the 'Clean Sweep' for the CTM." *The Other Side of Mexico*, no. 6 (July–Sept.): 8–9.

Whitehead, Laurence. 1980. "Mexico from Bust to Boom: A Political Evaluation of the 1976–1979 Stabilization Programme." *World Development* 8: 843–64.

————. 1989. "Political Change and Economic Stabilization: The 'Economic Solidarity Pact.'" In Cornelius, Gentleman, and Smith, eds.

————. N.d. "Mexico's Economic Prospects: Implications for State-Labor Relations." Mimeo.

Woldenberg M., José. 1980. "Notas sobre la burocracia sindical en México." *A: Revista de Ciencias Sociales y Humanidades* 1, 1 (September-December). Universidad Autónoma Metropolitana de Azcapotzalco.

Zapata, Francisco. 1981. "Mexico." In *International Handbook of Industrial Relations: Contemporary Developments and Research*, ed. Albert A. Blum. Westport, Conn.: Greenwood Press.

INDEX

Agrarian reform, 25, 29–30, 64, 98, 112
Agrarians, 16, 17, 20, 24
ALADI. *See* Asociación Latinoamericana de Integración
Alemán, Miguel, 33, 36, 40, 47, 55, 56
Alianza Revolucionaria Nacional (ARN), 20
Almazán, Juan Andreu, 29, 33
Alvarez, Luis, 150–51
Anarcho-syndicalism, 10
Argentina, 1, 47, 52, 81, 89, 136
ARN. *See* Alianza Revolucionaria Nacional
Asamblea Democrática para el Sufragio Efectivo, 113
Asociación Latinoamericana de Integración (ALADI), 134
Avila Camacho, Manuel, 27, 30, 33

Bloque de Unidad Obrera (BUO), 57–59
Brady Plan, 135
Brazil, 1, 47, 49, 52, 60, 81, 89, 92, 136
BUO. *See* Bloque de Unidad Obrera

Caciques, 53, 125. *See also Caudillos*
Calles, Plutarco Elías: and Cárdenas, 24–26, 29–31; in Maximato, 18–23, 39; under Obregón, 15–16, 18; presidency of, 14–18
Camacho, Manuel, 56
Canada, 134
Cananea Copper Mine, 139–40
Cárdenas, Cuauhtémoc, 139; and CD, 102–3, 107; and PRD, 129–31, 150; presidential candidacy of, 71, 74, 76–77, 110–17, 137
Cárdenas, Lázaro, 2, 9, 14, 19, 43, 64, 137; presidency of, 23–31
Cardenist (Cuauhtémoc) movement, 118, 123–24, 129–31, 135, 149–50, 157–58. *See also* Corriente Democrática (CD); Frente Democrático

Nacional (FDN); Partido de la Revolución Democrática (PRD)
Carr, Barry, 16, 63
Carranza, Venustiano, 14, 15
Carreño Carlón, José, 141
Castañeda, Jorge, 107, 135, 165
Castillo, Heberto, 112–13
Castro, Fidel, 65
Catholic Church, 17–18, 29, 32, 96
Caudillismo, 141
Caudillos, 19, 21, 24. *See also Caciques*
CCE, 93, 110
CD. *See* Corriente Democrática
Central Nacional de Trabajadores (CNT), 57, 59
CGOCM. *See* Confederación General de Obreros y Campesinos de México
CGT. *See* Confederación General de Trabajadores
Chamber of Deputies: in hegemonic party regime, 42, 68, 77; in 1980s, 87, 99–100, 114–17, 142–43, 149, 151, 162. *See also* Electoral reform; Electoral system
Charrazo, 44, 61
Charrismo, 35, 49, 51, 58, 60, 138
Chile, 1, 47, 49, 52, 60
Clientelism, 53, 104
CNAC. *See* Comité Nacional de Auscultacion y Coordinación
CNC. *See* Confederación Nacional Campesina
CNOP. *See* Confederación Nacional de Organizaciones Populares
CNT. *See* Central Nacional de Trabajadores *and* Confederación Nacional de Trabajadores
Coalition: in hegemonic party regime, 38, 52–54, 69; reconstitution of, 35, 71–78, 81, 89, 96–97, 108, 120, 128, 144, 147; of the whole, 4, 7, 37, 39,

RUTH BERINS COLLIER is Associate Professor of Political
Science at the University of California at Berkeley.

INTERNATIONAL AND AREA STUDIES
University of California at Berkeley

2223 Fulton Street, 3d floor   Berkeley, California 94720

Albert Fishlow, *Dean*

Recent books published by International and Area Studies include:

RESEARCH SERIES

71. *State & Welfare, USA/USSR: Contemporary Policy & Practice.*
    Eds. Gail W. Lapidus & Guy E. Swanson. $22.50

72. *The Politics of Debt in Argentina, Brazil, & Mexico.*
    Robert R. Kaufman. $9.50

73. *No Longer an American Lake? Alliance Problems in the South Pacific.*
    Ed. John Ravenhill. $14.95

74. *Thinking New about Soviet "New Thinking."*
    V. Kubálková & A. A. Cruickshank. $11.50

75. *Iberian Identity: Essays on the Nature of Identity in Portugal & Spain.*
    Eds. Richard Herr & John H. R. Polt. $17.50

76. *Argentine Unions, the State & the Rise of Perón, 1930–1945.*
    Joel Horowitz. $16.95

77. *The New Europe Asserts Itself: A Changing Role in International*
    Relations. Eds. Beverly Crawford & Peter W. Schulze. $19.95

78. *The Soviet Sobranie of Laws: Problems of Codification and*
    Non-Publication. Eds. Richard Buxbaum & Kathryn Hendley. $16.95

79. *Multilateralism in NATO: Shaping the Postwar Balance of Power,*
    1945–1961. Steve Weber. $9.50

80. *Beyond the Cold War: Conflict & Cooperation in the Third World.*
    Eds. George W. Breslauer, Harry Kreisler, & Benjamin Ward. $19.95

81. *Contemporary Catalonia in Spain and Europe.*
    Ed. Milton M. Azevedo. $13.50

INSTITUTE OF INTERNATIONAL STUDIES
POLICY PAPERS IN INTERNATIONAL AFFAIRS

35. *Large-Scale Foreign Policy Change: The Nixon Doctrine as History*
    & Portent. Earl C. Ravenal. $8.50

36. *The Internationalization of Japan's Security Policy: Challenges &*
    Dilemmas for a Reluctant Power. Michael G. L'Estrange. $5.95

37. *Why We Need Ideologies in U.S. Foreign Policy: Democratic Politics*
    & World Order. Edward H. Alden & Franz Schurmann. $8.50

38. *Vanguard Parties & Revolutionary Change in the Third World: Soviet*
    Perspectives & Their Implications. David E. Albright. $9.50

39. *Lessons of the Gulf War: Ascendant Technology and Declining Capability.*
    Gene I. Rochlin and Chris C. Demchak. $5.50

40. *Impediments on Environmental Policy-Making and Implementation in Central
    and Eastern Europe: Tabula Rasa vs. Legacy of the Past.* Peter Hardi. $6.50

INSIGHTS IN INTERNATIONAL AFFAIRS SERIES

1. *Confrontation in the Gulf: University of California Professors Talk about
   the War.* Ed. Harry Kreisler. $7.95

INSTITUTE OF EAST ASIAN STUDIES
RESEARCH PAPERS AND POLICY STUDIES

33. *U.S.-Thailand Relations in a New International Era.*
    Eds. Clark Neher and Wiwat Mungkandi. $20.00

34. *Korea-U.S. Relations in a Changing World.*
    Eds. Robert Sutter and Han Sungjoo. $20.00

35. *Japan, ASEAN, and the United States.*
    Eds. Harry H. Kendall and Clara Joewono. $20.00

36. *Asia in the 1990s: American and Soviet Perspectives.*
    Eds. Robert A. Scalapino and Gennady I. Chufrin. $20.00

KOREA RESEARCH MONOGRAPHS

16. *North Korea in Transition.*
    Eds. Chong-Sik Lee and Yoo Se-Hee. $12.00

CHINA RESEARCH MONOGRAPHS

36. *China's Education Reform in the 1980s: Policies, Issues, and Historical
    Perspectives.* Suzanne Pepper. $12.00

37. *Building a Nation-State: China after Forty Years.*
    Ed. Joyce K. Kallgren. $12.00

INDOCHINA RESEARCH MONOGRAPHS

5. *The Bunker Papers: Reports to the President from Vietnam, 1967–1973.*
   Ed. Douglas Pike.   (3 vols.) $35.00

CENTER FOR SLAVIC AND EAST EUROPEAN STUDIES
BERKELEY-STANFORD PROGRAM IN SOVIET STUDIES

*Analyzing the Gorbachev Era: Working Papers of the Students of the
Berkeley-Stanford Program.* $8.00

Can Gorbachev's Reforms Succeed?
Ed. George W. Breslauer. $12.95

*Steeltown, USSR: Glasnost, Destalinization & Perestroika in the
Provinces.* Stephen Kotkin. $6.00